AIR FRANCE

MIDLAND
An imprint of
Ian Allan Publishing

F-BOJB

AIR FRANCE

Geoff Jones

Acknowledgements

Many friends, acquaintances and others have helped with material for this book. Particular thanks go to Mike Hooks and John Underwood who so generously delved into their extensive photo libraries and loaned valuable, often previously unpublished, images. A host of other contributors include AENA, Airbus (Françoise Maenhaut at Media Relations), Air France Museum (Aline Maigne and Pascale Monmarson – more information at www.airfrancemusee.org), Norman Barfield (Vickers Viscount specialist), Tony Carless, Don Conway, Tony Dixon, Caroline Fontaine (Air France Press Office), Jennifer M. Gradidge, Nigel LePaige, William Lobet (ex-Air Inter), Gerry Manning, Robert O'Brien, George Pennick, Arthur J. Pullin, Rod Simpson, Mark Wagner (Aviation-Images.com) and John Wegg. Also, grateful thanks to Valerie, my wife, and Siân, my daughter, in the hope that by the date of publication she will have recovered from the serious injuries she sustained in an accident in February 2008.

The Air France Museum – whose staff helped considerably with this publication – was formed in 1972 at the instigation of Georges Galichon, then president of the Amicale des Anciens d'Air France. Its purpose is to gather together all documents relating to Air France and its many constituent companies. It has published many posters and postcards from the past, and images (paintings) of aircraft used by the company and its predecessors back as far as 1909. These works include those by famous contemporary French artists such as Albert Brenet, Paul Lengellé, Philippe Mitschké, Lucio Perinotto and James Prunier – some of these are reproduced in this book with the kind permission of the Musée. The museum has an extensive picture library and has helped with the publication of many books, such as this one, since its foundation. Musée Air France is located in central Paris close to the Champs-Elysées and Concorde district but on the opposite side of the River Seine; it is close to the Invalides metro station and beneath Air France's central Paris terminal, its Aérogare. Normal opening hours are 10.00 to 17.30 Monday to Friday. (See www.airfrancemusee.org for more details and listing of the merchandise it has on sale or telephone +33 (0)1 43.17.20.96, Fax +33 (0)1 40.62.91.27

Key to Photographic Credits

AFM – Air France Museum
AJP – Arthur J. Pullin
NB – Norman Barfield
AIC – Tony Carless
DC – Don Conway
JMG – Jennifer M. Gradidge
GPJ – Geoffrey P. Jones
GPJ Collection – Geoff Jones Collection
GP – George Pennick
JU – John Underwood
MJH – Mike Hooks
RoB – Bob O'Brien
MW – Mark Wagner/Aviation-Images.com

First published 2008

ISBN 978 1 85780 285 6

Published by Midland Publishing

An imprint of Ian Allan Publishing, Riverdene Business Park, Molesey Road, Hersham, Surrey KT12 4RG

Printed by Ian Allan Printing Ltd, Riverdene Business Park, Molesey Road, Hersham, Surrey KT12 4RG

Code: 0805/B2

Visit the Ian Allan Publishing website at www.ianallanpublishing.co.uk

Cover: Air France Concorde after landing for the final time at Le Bourget, Paris, June 2003. (*Mark Wagner Aviation-Images.com*)

Half-title: Sud Aviation SE210 Caravelle III F-WHRA. The second Caravelle delivered to Air France (F-BHRB was the first, on 19 March 1959) during its first flight on 18 May 1958. (*JU*)

Title: Fine air-to-air portrait of Air France Boeing 727-228 F-BOJB in the classic 1950s and 1960s livery of white, dark blue and silver. Delivered to Air France in April 1968, this was its second 727, almost a month after its first. (*MJH*)

Contents

Introduction

Home-grown, familiar and comfortable: Air France is all of these things, so much so that it can all too easily be taken for granted in the hustle and bustle of Europe's international airports. Air France, with its partner airline KLM, is now the world's leading airline in terms of revenue income and Europe's leading airline in terms of passenger numbers. 2008 is Air France's 75th anniversary and the occasion offers the perfect opportunity to remember Air France's often overlooked history. Although it has carried its famous name for three-quarters of a century, Air France's pedigree goes back to the start of the century, the birth of powered flight and founding of Compagnie Générale Transaérienne (CGT) in 1909.

While the US was first to achieve many commercial aviation benchmarks – such as the world's first scheduled aeroplane service, Tampa to St Petersburg, Florida, in January 1914 – the pioneering spirit of the French had already established a place in aviation history. The Octave Chanute, Félix DuTemple (the first powered model aeroplane to make a successful sustained flight in 1857), Clément Ader, Henry Farman and, of course, Louis Blériot, all achieved considerable firsts before January 1914. The Wright brothers – two Americans generally credited with building the world's first successful aeroplane that first flew on 17 December 1903 – demonstrated their flying machine at Camp d'Auvours, France, in 1908, in order to assert their supremacy in endurance flying.

The French have always been a nation in love with aviation, and this is nowhere better represented than in the history of Air France, its people and aircraft. Names such as Juan Tripp (founder of Pan American Airlines) and Charles Lindbergh (first to fly a solo, non-stop flight across the Atlantic in 1927 in the *Spirit of St Louis*) are heralded as masters of aviation by public relations stateside, but flick through the pages of this book and witness the pioneering scheduled maritime commercial aviation feats of Air France and its predecessors, many of which pre-date and perhaps even outshine Pan American.

As early as 1935, Air France had an international network of routes that stretched from Paris, west to Santiago in Chile and east to Saigon in Indo-China. Their predecessors' seaplane terminal at Antibes, and later at Biscarrosse, became the focus of commercial seaplane activity in the 1920s and 1930s. Transatlantic flights (mainly crossing the South Atlantic) were by this time the norm rather than the exception. The need to connect with France's vast overseas 'empire' in Africa, the Far East, Caribbean and South America was the driving force behind these developments, in much the same way as for Great Britain's Imperial Airways, the Dutch airline KLM and, to a lesser extent, Lufthansa.

Many great names are associated with Air France and its predecessors, none more famous than Jean Mermoz, the pioneering pilot who, by 1933, had effectively opened up the South Atlantic route from Africa to Brazil and onwards to Argentina and Chile. Later Air France was blessed with airline 'mavericks' to match any other on the world stage: Max Hymans and, more recently, Henri Ziegler, to name but two.

Air France's diverse airliner fleet is described here. Yes, it bought American, but the Caravelle, Airbus and of course Concorde were products of the nation's vibrant aviation industry that has been at the forefront of innovation and development since the beginning of the twentieth century.

There have been many ups and downs at Air France – the 1990 mergers and agglomerations of famous French airlines Air Inter, Air Charter International and UTA (Union de Transports Aériens), the transition from nationalised, government-owned 'flag-carrier' to private airline on 25 July 1994 and

Jean-Cyril Spinetta, current President and CEO. (*Air France*)

the founding of airline alliance, SkyTeam on 22 June 2000 with Delta, Aeromexico and Korean Air.

The May 2004 Air France/KLM merger was probably the most significant in European, if not world, air transport history, creating the world's largest airline in terms of operating revenues. And the Air France/KLM partnership is also profitable, which cannot be said of many of the world's major airlines, particularly those in the US. As this book closes for press, the next major step in Air France's expanding influence is poised to take place, the possible acquisition of Italian national airline (and SkyTeam member) Air Italia.

Air France is a truly great and historic airline, its distinguished history recounted here in the English language for the very first time.

Geoff Jones
Guernsey, Channel Islands
February 2008

Farman 60 'Goliath' F-FHMU, the type used by Compagnie des Grands Express Aériens to inaugurate their first Paris to London commercial schedule after WWI in February 1919. (*MJH*)

1

1920s
The Birth of Air France

The first commercial flight in France after WWI took place on 8 February 1919 when a Farman 'Goliath' twin engine biplane of Lignes Farman departed Paris for London. It was only ten years after Louis Blériot's epoch-making first crossing of the English Channel by a powered aircraft. This 1919 flight was under the captaincy of Lucien Bossoutrot, carried eleven passengers and became the first commercial international flight in history. It took the Farman 'Goliath' two hours and thirty minutes to fly the 178 miles between the two capitals, flying at an altitude of 4,000ft.

1920s

EVEN BEFORE WWI, FRANCE'S EMBRYONIC COMMERCIAL AIRLINES HAD OPENED FOR BUSINESS. LA COMPAGNIE GÉNÉRALE TRANSAÉRIENNE (CGT) WAS ESTABLISHED IN 1909 AND MADE ITS FIRST 'ON-REQUEST' COMMERCIAL FLIGHTS THE FOLLOWING YEAR USING *ASTRA* DIRIGIBLES AT VARIOUS CITIES THROUGHOUT MAINLAND FRANCE AND ONE OR TWO 'ABROAD' INCLUDING LUCERNE IN SWITZERLAND. THE FIRST *ASTRA* FLEW ON 2 APRIL 1910. NAMED *VILLE DE PAU*, 60M IN LENGTH AND WITH A VOLUME OF 4,475M³, IT WAS POWERED BY A 90HP CLÉMENT BAYARD ENGINE, CRUISED AT 39MPH AND COULD CARRY FOURTEEN PASSENGERS. ITS NAME WAS CHANGED TO *VILLE DE LUCERNE* FOLLOWING ITS SWISS FLIGHTS.

CGT also inaugurated seaplane services, the first of which took place on 22 March 1913 carrying two passengers in an Astra 'hydroplane' powered with a 100hp Renault in-line engine. The first flight was between the French Riviera cities of Nice, Cannes and Monte Carlo. Again the flights were 'on request' with the fare for each journey being 250 gold francs. The service was maintained until the outbreak of WWI in 1914. Post-war, CGT acquired a fleet of seven

Nieuport 30Ts that could carry between six and eight passengers at a speed of 90mph. In 1919, they inaugurated their first Paris to London scheduled passenger air service, operating alongside Lignes Farman. In 1921, they merged

Below: Painting of Hydroaéroplane Astra operated by Compagnie Générale Transaérienne on services between Nice-Cannes and Nice-Monte Carlo from 22 March 1913. (*Albert Brenet & AFM*)

with Messageries Aériennes, and retained the Paris-London service until 1922. CGT also flew Potez IX biplanes on these early Paris-London scheduled flights, a type used by sister company Compagnie Franco-Roumaine (CFR) on flights linking Paris, Strasbourg, Prague and Warsaw. They were also flying a Paris to Budapest route. CFR changed its name to Compagnie Internationale de Navigation Aérienne (CIDNA) in 1925, one of the main constituent airlines that helped form Air France in 1933.

On Christmas Day 1918, Pierre-Georges Latécoère made an inaugural flight from Toulouse to Barcelona under the name Lignes Latécoère, using a Salmson 2A2 biplane (F-ALAO) with a 280hp Salmson engine and carrying two passengers. This airline was bought out by Marcel Bouilloux-Lafont in 1927 and re-named Compagnie Générale Aéropostale.

The opening up of commercial air routes from France really started in the 1920s. Maurice Noguès was one of the pioneer pilots of the time. In 1925 he piloted his CIDNA (Compagnie Internationale de Navigation Aérienne) Blériot Spad 46 on a pioneering flight between Paris and Tehran, Iran. Prior to this in 1922, CFR – a predecessor of CIDNA –

'Headquarters' of CMA (Compagnie des Messageries Aériennes) after its foundation in 1919 by the 'three Louis' – Blériot, Bréguet and Renault. Using Morane, Farman, Caudron and Loiré aircraft, CMA proposed services from Paris to London, and from Lyons to Marseilles, Geneva and even on to Algeria using a Bréguet 'Goliath'. (*GPJ Collection*)

had established an important air link from Paris to Constantinople (Istanbul), via Strasbourg, Prague, Vienna, Budapest and Bucharest.

Air Union – formed from a merger of Compagnie des Messageries Aériennes and Compagnie des Grands Express Aériens – flew a variety of biplane types on scheduled services within France and internationally, the Blériot Spad 33 *Herbemont* with its 260hp Salmson 1 engine being able to carry four passengers over a sector length of 600+ miles. These were used on the Paris to London service (Le Bourget airport was the Paris terminal then), but were supplemented by the six-passenger, 100mph Blériot Spad 56/4 biplanes around 1925. CMA also used Bréguet XIVs on its Paris, Lille, Brussels and Amsterdam schedule.

Meanwhile back in the Mediterranean, Air Union and Société Maritime de Transports Aériens Aéronavale –

Aéronavale for short – were establishing the first scheduled flying boat (hydroplane) services based at Antibes (located between Cannes and Nice). Air Union commissioned Donnet-Denhaut to build a passenger-carrying seaplane, the HB.3, to initiate service from Antibes to Tunisia via Ajaccio in Corsica; it flew the first Antibes to Ajaccio route in 1921, but the aircraft did not have the safe range to reach Tunisia. The HB.3's 275hp Hispano-Suiza did not provide enough power either and the service with the HB.3 was abandoned. A similar type, known as the Schreck FBA 19 HMT.3 was designed and built in 1925 with a more powerful 350hp Hispano-Suiza engine, Air Union using it (F-AHCY) for an experimental flight between Paris and London where it landed on the River Thames. Aéronavale were more successful, using their twin-engine Lioré et Olivier LéO 13 (F-AFDJ and F-AHAD) to inaugurate a new Antibes to Ajaccio schedule on 16 May 1923, carrying four passengers at a speed of 70mph.

The LéO 13 design paved the way for many new developments such as the LéO 198 which was used by

Breguet 14 F-JAGB of Les Messageries Aériennes in 1919. (JU)

associate company, Jean-Paul Piaz's Société Transatlantique Aérienne (STA), to make the first commercial transatlantic flight on 13 August 1928, the LéO 198 being catapulted from the steam ship *Ile-de-France* as part of the ingenious planning to establish this air service. The idea of combining ship-borne transport and an aircraft enabled STA to cut a whole 24 hours from the normal all-ship, transatlantic mail delivery service from France (Le Havre) to the USA (New York). The aircraft was launched when the ship was 465 miles from New York, to which it then flew, landing on the Hudson River. The service was suspended for a while, but resumed in 1930 with a CAMS 37 seaplane, occasionally flying a mix of mail and passengers. Then in 1932, when the 30-knot steam ship *Normandie* was launched and entered the transatlantic market, mail deliveries between France and the USA took only 4.5 days, so the gains from ship-borne aircraft became minimal and the service was abandoned.

CIDNA meanwhile, using a variety of esoteric Farman designed airliners, including the first monoplane, the Farman F.4A Jabiru in 1925, were opening up new scheduled passenger routes, replacing those flown by CFR. The Farman F.4X Jabiru was a tri-motor, which used three 300hp Salmson radials and could carry six passengers at speeds up to 110mph. The Jabiru was used to fly between Paris and Zurich. Like many of the aircraft designs of the time the passengers were in an enclosed cabin, but the pilots were seated above and at the front of the aircraft in open cockpits. The similar, but single engine, eight-passenger Farman F170 Jabiru, introduced in 1926, was similar in concept to the F.4X.

The pioneering flights to West Africa and onward to South America by Jean Mermoz are part of French folklore. Flying Lignes Latécoère Bréguet XIV and, later, Compagnie Générale Aéropostale Latécoère 25 and 26 aircraft, Mermoz

made his historic flights between 1926 and 1929. Mermoz earned media acclaim in France akin to that of Lindbergh in the USA, his pioneering flights being followed religiously by the French press and public. Henri Guillaumet followed in Mermoz's footsteps with his postal flights for Aéropostale, flying Potez 25s. Mermoz's flights inspired the works of author Saint-Exupéry, such as *Wind, Sand and Stars*.

On the other side of the world Compagnie Air Asie (formed in 1928) were also using LéO 198s to open up air services from 1929 onwards. The LéO 198 could land on the numerous rivers in the Indo-China region and operated a regular service between Vinh and Canton. By the end of 1929, Air Asie had Potez 32s in service on their Bangkok to

Near-disaster at Croydon when a CGEA Farman 60 'Goliath' *Normandie* (F-AECU) overran the airfield on landing, ploughed through the perimeter fence and on to the main road. (*MJH*)

Saigon service, but in 1930 merged with rival airline, Compagnie Air Union-Lignes d'Orient (AULO), to form Air Orient. In July 1932 Air Orient inaugurated services with their Fokker VII b.3ms between Damascus, Saigon and Hanoi, flying via Iraq, Iran, India, Burma, Thailand and the former French Indo-China. The service was flown once a week, the first part of the service from Marseilles to Beirut being flown by CAMS 53 seaplanes. The passengers transferred from Beirut to Damascus over land. Air Union was another of the airlines that came together in 1933 to form Air France.

With developments in airliner design and construction, France's domestic and international services burgeoned. Air Union put their first 18 passenger Lioré et Olivier LéO 213 *Rayon d'Or* twin-engine biplanes into service in 1928 on their Paris to London and then Paris-Lyons-Marseilles services. This was state of the art air travel, the 'luxurious'

LéO 213 also being equipped with a 12-seat airliner restaurant on board.

France's status as the birthplace of aviation, specifically commercial aviation, may be disputed by other countries, but it can be shown beyond doubt that French pioneers and their world-beating aircraft laid the foundations for all aspects of aerospace development and in particular the formation of commercial passenger air transport, resulting in the emergence of its very epitome, Air France, in 1933.

In 1923, Compagnie des Grands Express Aériens (CGEA) merged with Compagnie Messageries Aériennes (CMA) to become Air Union. Albert Gauchet became Director General of the new airline (seen here shaking hands) and went on to become an important figure in the formation of Air France in 1933. (*GPJ Collection*)

Cie des Grandes
Express Aériens.
Poster dating
from 1920.
(*AFM*)

C^{eo} Franco-
Roumaine de
Navigation
Aériennes.
Poster from
1922. (*AFM*)

Above: Founded in 1920 in Bucharest, Romania, was Compagnie Franco-Roumaine de Navigation Aérienne. One of their Potez VIIs (probably F-FRAA) is seen here on arrival of its first flight from Bucharest to London (Croydon) in October 1920 – it carried just two passengers in tandem behind the pilot. In 1925, the airline changed ownership and its name, becoming Compagnie Internationale de Navigation Aérienne (CIDNA), one of the original companies to form Air France in 1933. (*MJH*)

Below and Right: Blériot 115 *Roland Garros* in 1924. (*Maxim Prieur via JU*)

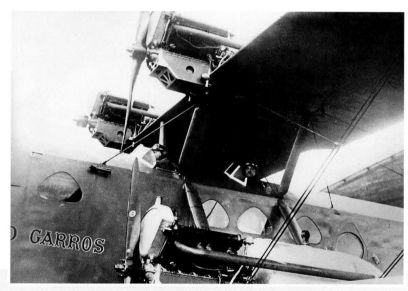

Right and Below:
Blériot Spad 33
F-ACMD of
Compagnie des
Messageries
Aériennes pictured
in 1924 and
similar to the
CIDNA aircraft
flown by Maurice
Noguès in 1925 on
route proving
flights to
inaugurate air
services from Paris
to Tehran, Iran.
(*MJH*)

Left: Lignes Latécoère (CGEA) Bréguet XIV at Cap Juby in West Africa with (left to right) Louis Pichard (Chief Mechanic), Pierre Picard, Jean Mermoz and M. Bougneres in 1926. (*AFM*)

Below: Interior of a CIDNA Blériot Spad 56/4 as used by several French airlines in the mid-1920s. (*MJH*)

Lignes
Aériennes
G.Latécoère.
Poster from
1921. (*AFM*)

Left: Bernard 190T F-AJLA pictured over the hangars at Le Bourget in 1929, operated by Compagnie Internationale de Navigation Aérienne (CIDNA). CIDNA was formed in 1925 when Compagnie Franco-Roumaine de Navigation Aérienne (CFR) changed its name and ownership. Started in 1920 on the initiative of Romanian banker Aristide Blank, a network of services was developed in Eastern Europe, as well as services between Paris and Strasbourg, Vienna, Belgrade, Budapest, Bucharest and Constantinople (Istanbul). CIDNA retained its Franco-Romanian network but diversified with new services to Basle, Zurich, Sofia and Salonika and became one of Air France's founding airline companies in 1933. The Bernard 190Ts had a 420hp Gnome-Rhône engine and could carry five to seven passengers at 125mph. (*GPJ Collection*)

Below: Latécoère Laté 26 F-AILR (c/n 667) with pioneering pilots Pivot, Moré and Macaigne, fourth person unidentified. With sixty of these aircraft, Aéropostale was able to pioneer its 1920s routes to Africa and South America. Photo taken *circa* 1928. (*GPJ Collection*)

Right: Latham L.1 (c/n 01) F-ESEJ, which was to have been flown by Alphonse Dehamel in the Cowes, Isle of Wight, Schneider Trophy Races of 1923; it was very similar in design to the Schreck FBA 19 HMT.3 that was used to pioneer early French international air service routes, including from Paris to London (River Thames). (*JU*)

Below: Latécoère Laté 25 F-AIEH in 1929 on arrival in Santiago, Chile, piloted by Jean Mermoz. (*AFM*)

Above: Bréguet 14T, probably F-CMAD, pictured at Croydon in 1924 and operated by Compagnie des Messageries Aériennes (CMA), which had been formed in 1919. (*MJH*)

Left: Farman 270, probably prototype F-AMAO, as used by Lignes Farman from 1919 until the 1922 formation of Société Générale de Transport Aérien (SGTA). The Farman, in a slightly re-modelled version, was known as the 'Goliath' and carried the first twelve passengers between Paris (Toussus-le-Noble) and London on 8 February 1919 with Captain Bossoutrot in charge. (*MJH*)

1920s

Right: Fokker V11 b.3m tri-motors were first used by Air Orient from July 1932 onwards, flying between Damascus (Syria) and Hanoi (French Indo-China, now Vietnam). They carried inspirational names such as *La Résolve* and *La Zélée* (F-ALSB, pictured). Air Union also used the seahorse or 'hippocampe' logo that was adopted by Air France in 1933 and used extensively up until the introduction of the new Air France livery in 1974. (*GPJ Collection*)

Below: Version of the Avion Bréguet 16 developed from a night bomber and similar to the Bréguet XIV used for civilian services in the 1920s, and particularly Lignes Latécoère aircraft flown by Jean Mermoz from March 1926 onwards on the Casablanca to Dakar leg of their African routes to Cap Juby. (*MJH*)

Air Union.
Poster
dating from
1929. (*AFM*)

Couzinet 71 *Arc-en-Ciel* F-AMBV of CGA on its inaugural flight to South America, seen on arrival in Rio de Janeiro in January 1933, flown by Jean Mermoz. (*AFM*)

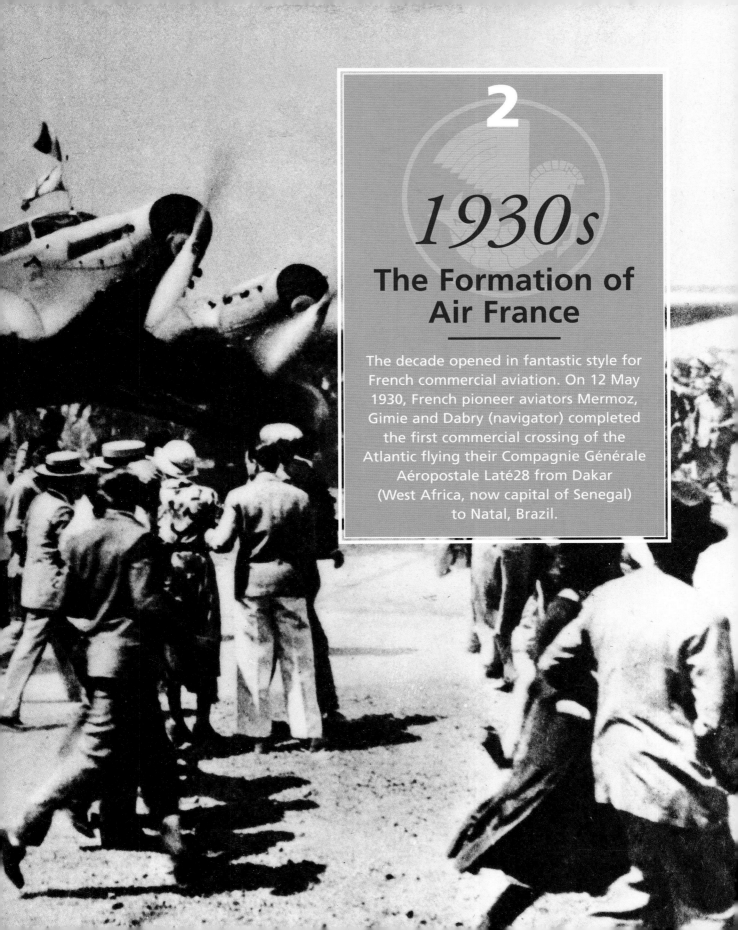

2

1930s
The Formation of Air France

The decade opened in fantastic style for French commercial aviation. On 12 May 1930, French pioneer aviators Mermoz, Gimie and Dabry (navigator) completed the first commercial crossing of the Atlantic flying their Compagnie Générale Aéropostale Laté28 from Dakar (West Africa, now capital of Senegal) to Natal, Brazil.

1930s

THEY SET OFF FROM TOULOUSE WITH 128KG (280LB) OF MAIL, BEARING FOR THE FIRST TIME THE TRICOLOUR 'PAR AVION' STICKERS THAT SOON BECAME SYNONYMOUS WITH RAPID DELIVERIES. JEAN DABRY WENT ON TO COMPLETE MORE THAN FIVE HUNDRED AND EIGHTY ATLANTIC CROSSINGS FOR AIR FRANCE AND ITS PREDECESSORS, IN AIRCRAFT RANGING FROM THE LATÉ28 TO THE LOCKHEED SUPER CONSTELLATION. HE ACHIEVED HIS 500TH CROSSING IN AIR FRANCE'S SILVER JUBILEE YEAR IN 1958.

Following this flight across the southern Atlantic, on 2 September 1930, French aviators Dieudonné Coste and Maurice Bellonte made the first westbound, non-stop crossing of the North Atlantic between Paris and New York (Valley Stream, Long Island) in a time of 37 hours and 18 minutes opening up the possibilities for commercial services on this route. In 1935, Air France purchased Air Bleu (the national mail carrier), and in 1937 started serious exploration of commercial North Atlantic air services, establishing a subsidiary, Air France Transatlantique.

On 21 July 1936, at Dakar (St Louis), Air France was able to celebrate the 10th anniversary of regular mail flights from France to West Africa, as major modernisation programmes got under way on existing aircraft, particularly with new 'blind-flying' equipment, radios and engines.

Three new types were also ordered in the middle of the decade, the Dewoitine D.338 tri-motor, the Bloch 220 – mainly for European services – and the high-wing Potez 62 for South American services between Buenos Aires, Argentina, and Santiago, Chile. The latter type was also used in Europe and on Air France's Far East network.

France's colonies in south-east Asia were also a focus. In 1930, that pioneering French aviator, Maurice Noguès led an exploratory flight, prior to the establishment of commercial services, from France to Saigon. For his 1930 flight he flew a Farman 190, arriving in Saigon on 9 March. The following year scheduled services were started and

CAMS 53 F-ALCG (c/n 31) 'Timgad' with Aéropostale logo on the nose sometime around 1930/31. (*AFM*)

Right: Jean Brun (left), one of Air France's early pilots, pictured infront of a Farman F190 which flew with Lignes Farman's successor SGTA, fifteen aircraft being transferred to Air France's fleet in 1933. The Farman F190 was a significant aircraft when, in 1929, it broke records for Saigon to Paris and Paris to Madagascar flown by pioneering pilots such as Bailly, Réginensi and Marsot. Brun was awarded the Légion d'Honneur in May 1983 by President Mitterrand. (*GPJ Collection*)

twenty-two flights completed that year. By 1933, with the formation of Air France, several Bréguet 280T 'Saloon' aircraft were based in Saigon, where they remained in service until 1938.

Air travel was becoming more reliable and popular. In 1932, just before the formation of Air France, the constituent airlines carried 40,138 passengers, but by 1935, this figure had increased to 60,719. Post (mail) tonnage also increased for the same years from 177 to 271 tonnes. In 1938, Air France carried 104,000 passengers and flew 11 million kilometres with a fleet of forty-seven land planes and twelve seaplanes.

Air France's African network was also expanding its traditional coastal services down to Dakar and to the French territories of North Africa. In association with Air Afrique and Aéromaritime, services were being flown to the Congo, Chad and even Madagascar, albeit infrequently and driven mainly by postal delivery requirements.

Below: Air Union Farman 60 'Goliath' biplane F-AECU at London Croydon around 1932. Air Union was founded in 1923 following the merger of Messageries Aériennes and Grands Express Aériens. In 1926, Aéronavale also became part of Air Union, which was one of the five original airlines merged in 1933 to form Air France. (*MJH*)

Below: Max Hymans (1900-1961) poses with a
Wibault 282 T-12 (F-AKEK) at Vienna in May 1933,
the aircraft already wearing Air France titles. Hymans
became Air France's most enigmatic President, serving
from July 1948 to January 1961; from 1954 to 1955
he was also President of the newly formed International
Air Transport Association. (*GPJ Collection*)

Above: 4:00pm on 7 October 1933 at Paris Le Bourget, the official inauguration of Air France with government Minister for Air, Pierre Cot, officiating. Four aircraft were assembled wearing the new 'Air France' name, including the Wibault 283 T-12 *La Voile d'Or*, a Farman 303 and a Latécoère Laté 28-1, the mainstays of the new AF fleet. (*GPJ Collection*)

Aeropostale
poster dating
from 1930.
(*AFM*)

Left: Bréguet 530 *Saigon* F-AMSX ordered by Compagnie Air Union in 1933 and then transferred to Air France. (*JU*)

Below: Dewoitine D.332 (c/n 01) F-AMMY at London's Croydon airport in 1934 with other contemporary civil transports including KLM Fokker F.XII PH-AII (c/n 5301) and later G-ADZK. The other aircraft is AB Aerotransport Junkers W.33de SE-ABZ (c/n 2548). (*JU*)

Right and Below:
Blériot 5190 *Santos-Dumont France-Bresil* which made 38 mail flights across the South Atlantic between 1934 and 1937 with the unique three-engine, 4,650hp Hispano-Suiza, configuration. (*Musée de l'Air/JU*)

Left: Ten Wibault 283 T-12s were built specially for Air France in 1934, and fitted with three 350hp Gnome-Rhône engines with Ratier propellers. Pictured is F-AMTS *L'Infatigable* c/n 9. (*JU*)

Below: Two of Air France's early Presidents, Ernest Roume and Paul Tirard with other dignitaries in 1936 in front of the company's first Dewoitine D.338 F-AOZA. Note the signboard to the right of the entry door with the schedule – Paris, Brussels, Hamburg, Copenhagen, Stockholm. (*GPJ Collection*)

Above: The high-wing monoplane Potez 62 had two 870hp Gnome et Rhône radial engines but when the type was transferred (including F-ANQN) for Air France operations in South America and trans-Andean flights between Buenos Aires, Argentina, and Santiago, Chile, new in-line 720hp Hispano-Suiza engines were substituted. (*GPJ Collection*)

Below: Pictured at London's Croydon airport in company with a KLM DC-2, is the Potez 62 F-AOTU (c/n 15), which could carry fourteen or sixteen passengers. It had a retractable undercarriage and here with its two 870hp Gnome et Rhône radial engines could cruise at 170mph. (*MJH*)

Above: The first Dewoitine D.338 F-AOZA, *Clemence Isaure*, when first delivered to Air France in 1936. The three Hispano-Suiza engine airliner could seat between twelve and twenty-two passengers and carried four crew – pilot, radio operator, mechanic and barman! (*GPJ Collection*)

Left: Air France's new ticket sales office at Le Bourget opened on 4 September 1933, already illustrating the airline's worldwide network and the famous 'hippocampe' logo. (*AFM*)

Below and opposite bottom: Summer 1937 Paris-London timetable, 'The Golden Clipper' with a picture of a Wibault 283 T-12 on the cover. (*AFM*)

Opposite top and above: Successor to the smaller, eight to ten passenger Dewoitine 333, the Dewoitine D.338 was used extensively on Air France's European and inter-continental network including the first Paris to Hong Kong service in August 1938. The type also served with Lignes Aériennes Militaires (see Chapter 3), based in Damascus, Syria, and were still in Air France service up until 1947. (*GPJ Collection*)

THE GOLDEN CLIPPER

LIGNE **476**

PARIS - LONDRES

		31-5-37 2-10-37	Du 4 Avril 1937 au 2 Octobre 1937			
		S	S	D	S	D
PARIS 116, Rue Lafayette	dép.	7.25	9.55	12.25	15.25	17.25
LE BOURGET	dép.	8.00	10.30	13.00	16.00	18.00
CROYDON	arr.	9.30•	12.00•	14.30•	17.30•	19.30•
LONDRES 51a, Park Lane	arr.	10.30•	13.00•	15.30•	18.30•	20.30•

S - Semaine.   D - Quotidien Dimanche compris.
• Du 4 au 17 Avril, une heure plus tôt.

LONDRES - PARIS

		Du 4 Avril 1937 au 2 Octobre 1937			31-5-37 2-10-37	4-4-37 2-10-37
		S	D	D	S	S
LONDRES 51a, Park Lane	dép.	7.00•	9.30•	12.00•	15.00•	17.30•
CROYDON	dép.	8.00•	10.30•	13.00•	16.00•	18.30•
LE BOURGET	arr.	9.30	12.00	14.30	17.30	20.00
PARIS 116, Rue Lafayette	arr.	10.05	12.35	15.05	18.05	20.35

Les horaires et les tarifs sont susceptibles d'être modifiés sans préavis.

TARIFS

ALLER . . . . 425 frs
ALLER et { Validité : 15 jours . . . . 720 frs
RETOUR { — 60 jours . . . . 765 frs
WEEK-END (du Vendredi matin au Mardi soir) . . . . 595 frs
Demandez les billets de Week-End SANS PASSEPORT

EXCÉDENT DE BAGAGES : Franchise 15 kgs ; au dessus de ce poids : taxe de 2.50 par kilog. supplémentaire.

Arrival of the first Air France Bloch 220
aircraft at London's Croydon airport in
1937, F-AOHE (c/n 5) *Aunis*. (*MJH*)

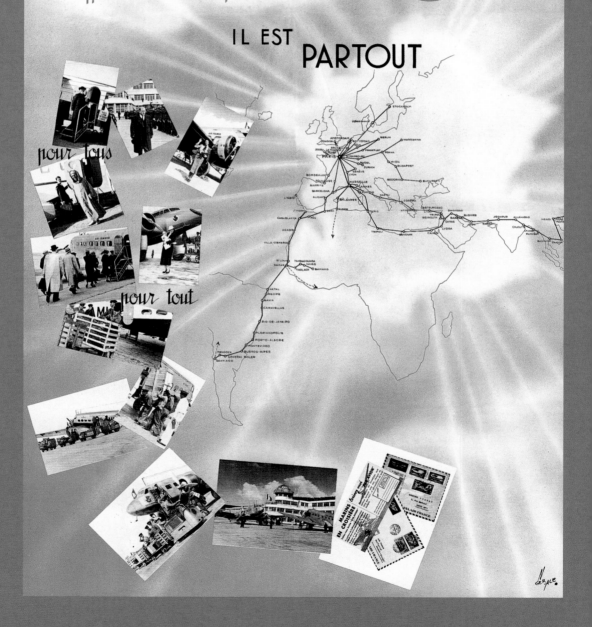

Air France 1937 worldwide route network and the aircraft used on specific routes (right). (*Editions Perceval + AFM*)

4 TYPES D'APPAREILS
UNE FLOTTE A HAUTES PERFORMANCES POUR UN RÉSEAU MONDIAL

LE PULLMANN EUROPÉEN

CARACTÉRISTIQUES TECHNIQUES

- BIMOTEUR GNOME-RHONE 14 N.
- PUISSANCE TOTALE 1840 CV.
- HÉLICES TRIPALES - PAS VARIABLE EN VOL.
- MONOPLAN MÉTALLIQUE.
- ENVERGURE : 22 M. 72.
- POIDS TOTAL : 9 TONNES.
- VITESSE DE CROISIÈRE : 300 KMS-H.
- RAYON D'ACTION : 1.000 KMS.
- TRAIN ESCAMOTABLE.
- DISPOSITIFS HYPERSUSTENTATEURS.

STOCKHOLM 6 H.
COPENHAGUE 3 H. 45
AMSTERDAM 2 H.
BRUXELLES 1 H.
LONDRES 1 H. 15   BERLIN 4 H. 30
PARIS   VARSOVIE 6 H. 25
STRASBOURG 1 H. 30
PRAGUE 3 H. 45
VIENNE 5 H.
BUDAPEST 8 H. 10
LYON 1 H. 35   BELGRADE 7 H. 40
BUCAREST 9 H. 40
GENÈVE 1 H. 50
BALE 1 H. 40
MARSEILLE 2 H. 30   ZURICH 2 H. 10
CANNES 3 H. 30
BORDEAUX 2 H. 15
BIARRITZ 3 H. 15

CARACTÉRISTIQUES COMMERCIALES

ÉQUIPAGE : 1 PILOTE CHEF DE BORD, 1 RADIO, 1 BARMAN.

- 2 CABINES - 16 PLACES.
- FAUTEUILS SOUPLES.
- TABLETTES POUR LUNCH.
- CABINE INSONORISÉE ET CLIMATISÉE.
- AÉRATION ET ÉCLAIRAGE INDIVIDUELS.
- BAR - BUFFET FROID.
- ÉMISSION ET RÉCEPTION DE RADIOGRAMMES.
- TOILETTE.
- SOUTES A BAGAGES.

17 BLOCH 220

L'AVION GRAND TRANSPORT

CARACTÉRISTIQUES COMMERCIALES

ÉQUIPAGE : 1 PILOTE CHEF DE BORD, 1 RADIO, 1 MÉCANICIEN, 1 BARMAN.

2 CABINES :
- RÉSEAU CONTINENTAL : 22 PLACES.
- D'AFRIQUE : 15 PLACES ALLONGÉES.
- D'ORIENT : 12 PLACES ALLONGÉES.

FAUTEUILS SOUPLES A DOSSIER MOBILE (pour Afrique et Orient seulement)
- TABLES POUR LUNCH.
- CABINE INSONORISÉE ET CLIMATISÉE.
- AÉRATION ET ÉCLAIRAGE INDIVIDUELS.
- BAR BUFFET FROID ET CHAUD.
- TOILETTE.
- SOUTE A BAGAGES.
  - RÉSEAU CONTINENTAL
  - RÉSEAU D'AFRIQUE
  - RÉSEAU D'ORIENT.

PARIS
2 H. 40 TOULOUSE
BARCELONE 3 H. 30
CASABLANCA 10 H. 30
DAKAR 22 H.

MARSEILLE 2 H. 30
TUNIS   NAPLES
TRIPOLI   CORFOU
LE CAIRE   ATHÈNES
DAMAS (2ᵐᵉ jour)
BAGDAD
BASSORAH
BOUCHIR
JASK
KARACHI (3ᵐᵉ jour)
JODHPUR
ALLAHABAD
CALCUTTA (4ᵐᵉ jour)
AKYAB
RANGOON
BANGKOK (5ᵐᵉ jour)
SAIGON
HANOI
HONG-KONG (6ᵐᵉ jour)

CARACTÉRISTIQUES TECHNIQUES

- TRIMOTEUR HISPANO-SUIZA 9 V.
- PUISSANCE TOTALE : 1980 CV.
- HÉLICES TRIPALES - PAS VARIABLE EN VOL.
- MONOPLAN MÉTALLIQUE.
- ENVERGURE : 29 M. 38.
- POIDS TOTAL : 11 TONNES.
- VITESSE DE CROISIÈRE : 290 KMS-H.
- RAYON D'ACTION : 2.000 KMS.
- TRAIN ESCAMOTABLE.
- DISPOSITIFS HYPERSUSTENTATEURS.

28 DEWOITINE 338

LE PAQUEBOT VOLANT

CARACTÉRISTIQUES TECHNIQUES

- QUADRIMOTEUR HISPANO-SUIZA 12 X.
- PUISSANCE TOTALE : 2.880 CV.
- HÉLICES TRIPALES - PAS VARIABLE EN VOL.
- HYDRAVION A COQUE MÉTALLIQUE ET AILE HAUTE.
- VOILURE CONSTRUCTION BOIS.
- ENVERGURE : 31 M. 800.
- POIDS TOTAL : 13 TONNES.
- RAYON D'ACTION : 1.000 KMS.
- BALLONNETS STABILISATEURS.
- DISPOSITIFS HYPERSUSTENTATEURS.
- VITESSE DE CROISIÈRE : 270 KMS H.

PARIS
MARSEILLE
AJACCIO 2 H.
ALGER 5 H.
TUNIS 6 H.

CARACTÉRISTIQUES COMMERCIALES

ÉQUIPAGE : 1 PILOTE, CHEF DE BORD, 1 RADIO-TÉLÉGRAPHISTE, 1 MÉCANICIEN NAVIGANT, 1 BARMAN.

- 2 CABINES POUR 14 ET 12 PASSAGERS.
- FAUTEUILS SOUPLES A DOSSIER MOBILE.
- CABINES INSONORISÉES ET CLIMATISÉES.
- BAR - BUFFET FROID ET CHAUD.
- TOILETTE.
- SOUTES A BAGAGES.
- SERVICES QUOTIDIENS SUR : MARSEILLE-AJACCIO-TUNIS. MARSEILLE-ALGER.

7 LéO 246

LE RACER TRANSATLANTIQUE

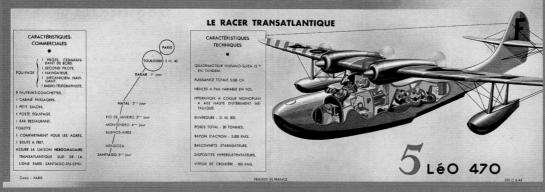

CARACTÉRISTIQUES COMMERCIALES

ÉQUIPAGE : 1 PILOTE, COMMANDANT DE BORD, 1 SECOND PILOTE, 1 NAVIGATEUR, 1 MÉCANICIEN NAVIGANT, 1 RADIO-TÉLÉGRAPHISTE.

- 8 FAUTEUILS-COUCHETTES.
- 1 CABINE PASSAGERS.
- 1 PETIT SALON.
- 1 POSTE ÉQUIPAGE.
- 1 BAR-RESTAURANT.
- TOILETTE.
- 1 COMPARTIMENT POUR LES AGRÈS.
- 1 SOUTE A FRET.
- ASSURE LA LIAISON HEBDOMADAIRE TRANSATLANTIQUE SUD DE LA LIGNE PARIS - SANTIAGO-DU-CHILI.

PARIS
TOULOUSE 2 H. 40
DAKAR 1ᵉʳ jour
NATAL 2ᵐᵉ jour
RIO DE JANEIRO 3ᵐᵉ jour
MONTÉVIDÉO 4ᵐᵉ jour
BUENOS-AIRES
MENDOZA
SANTIAGO 5ᵐᵉ jour

CARACTÉRISTIQUES TECHNIQUES

- QUADRIMOTEUR HISPANO-SUIZA 12 Y EN TANDEM.
- PUISSANCE TOTALE 3.500 CV.
- HÉLICES A PAS VARIABLE EN VOL.
- HYDRAVION A COQUE MONOPLAN A AILE HAUTE ENTIÈREMENT MÉTALLIQUE.
- ENVERGURE : 31 M. 800.
- POIDS TOTAL : 20 TONNES.
- RAYON D'ACTION : 3.500 KMS.
- BALLONNETS STABILISATEURS.
- DISPOSITIFS HYPERSUSTENTATEURS.
- VITESSE DE CROISIÈRE : 350 KMS.

5 LéO 470

Océo - PARIS   PRINTED IN FRANCE   519 C 6 AF

Above: Air France Bloch 220 F-AOHB (c/n 2) *Gascogne*. The type first flew in 1935, but entered service with Air France in 1937 on its main inter-European city routes. It could cruise at 175mph (280km/h), powered by two 830hp Gnome-Rhône engines. (*GPJ Collection*)

Right: Interior of an Air France Bloch 220, the wing spar creating a huge step across the central aisle in the forefront of the photo. The Bloch 220 could seat sixteen passengers. It was in a Bloch 220 that the Président du Conseil Edouard Daladier flew to Munich in September 1938 for talks with Adolf Hitler. (*MJH*)

Left: Inauguration of the first regular post and parcel air service between Paris-Lyons-Marseilles-Côte d'Azur on 16 February 1938 (see Chapter 3 also). Pictured in Paris, the mail is loaded aboard Air France Bloch 220 F-AOHE *Saintonge* amidst much media attention. (*GPJ Collection*)

Below: Four engine F-APUZ Farman 2231 named *Chef Pilote Laurent Guerrero*, which achieved fame in November 1937, when pilots Paul Codos and Marcel Reine broke the Paris-Santiago (Chile) record in a time of 58 hours 41 minutes. This 175mph aircraft was requisitioned at the outbreak of WWII and destroyed in a take-off accident at Dakar on 11 Dec 1939. The Farman 2231 was derived from Air France's two mail service aircraft, the Farman 2200 and 2220. (*GPJ Collection*)

Above: Laté 521 *Lieutenant de Vaisseau Paris* in 1938 before it was registered as F-NORD. (*JU*)

Below: Air France 1938/39 worldwide route network stretching from Hong Kong in the East to Santiago, Chile, in the West. (*Editions Perceval + AFM*)

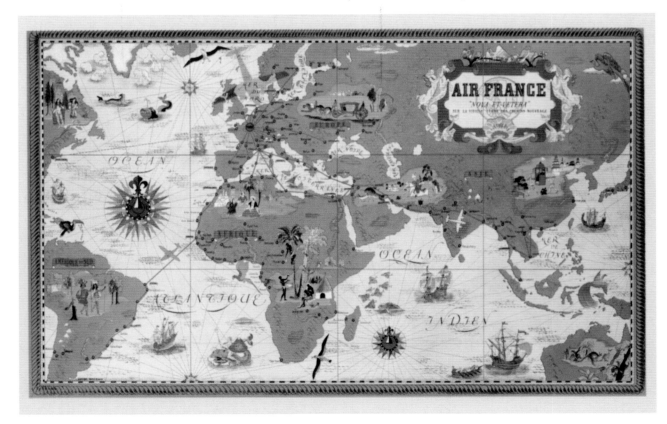

Above: Laté 522 *Ville de Saint-Pierre* F-ARAP in April 1939. (*Musée de l'Air/JU*)

Left: Four-engine (720hp Hispano-Suiza) Lioré et Olivier Léo H.246 F-AREL, one of seven built as replacements for the LéO H.242s on Air France's Marseilles to Algiers route, pictured in October 1939. (*Musée de l'Air/JU*)

Winter timetable 1938/39
Paris/London to Hong Kong.
(*AFM*)

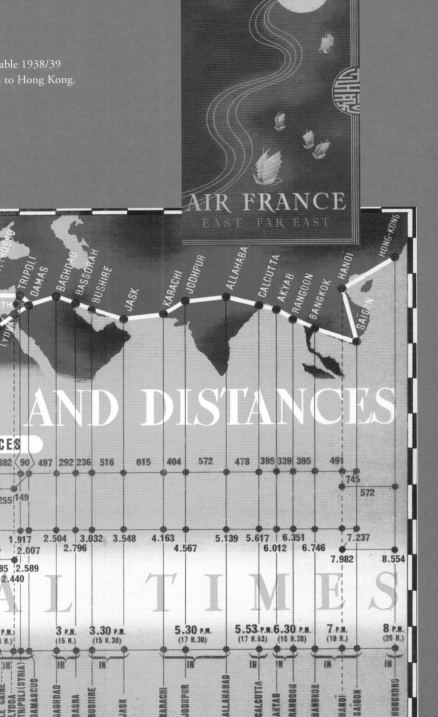

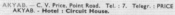

OFFICES AND AGENCIES

AIR FRANCE
Central Administrative Offices
2, Rue Marbeuf (Paris 8e): Tél.: Élysées 20-60, 38-95

AKYAB. — C. V. Price, Point Road. Tel. : 7. Telegr. : PRICE AKYAB. - **Hotel : Circuit House.**

ALLAHABAD. — Steele & Cⁱᵉ, 8, Stratchey road. Tel. : 367. Telegr. : STEELE ALLAHABAD. - **Alliance Hotel.**

ATHENS (Athenai) — Air France, 4, rue du Stade, Nᵒ 7, 3rd floor. Tel. : 21-674, 82-116. Telegr. : AIRFRANS ATHENS. — Wagons-Lits/Cook, place Syntagmatos. Tel. : 30-381. Telegr. : SLEEPING ATHENS. - **Hotel Grande-Bretagne & King George Hotel.**

BAGHDAD (Bagdad). — AIR FRANCE, Airport. Tel.: 1-42. Telegr. : AIRFRANS BAGHDAD. - **Hotel Zia & Hotel Maude.**

BANGKOK. — Aerial Transport Cy of Siam Ltd. Airway House. Tel. : 30971. Telegr. AIRFRANS BANGKOK. - **Trocadero Hotel.**

BASRA. — Impérial Airways, Airport. Tel. : 06385. Telegr. : AIRWAYS BASRA - **Shatt el Arab Hotel.**

BEIRUT. — Wagons-Lits/Cook, rue Allenby. Tel. : 66-62. Telegr. : SLEEPING BEIRUT. - **Hotel Saint-Georges.**

BUSHIRE. — Tejaratkhaneh S.M.H., Kazerooni & Sons. Telegr. : AIRFRANS BUSHIRE. - **Hotel : Airways Rest House.**

CALCUTTA. — Volkart Brothers, Clive Buildings, Block A, 8 Clive Street. Tel. : 1151. Telegr. : VOLKART CALCUTTA. - **The Great Eastern Hotel.**

CORFU. — Air France, Phaïakon Airport. Telegr. : AIRFRANS CORFU. - **Hotel Belle Venise.**

DAMASCUS. — Air France, 30, avenue Fouad-Iᵉʳ. Tel. : 12-20. Telegr. : AIRFRANS DAMASCUS. - **Hotel Omayad and Orient Palace Hotel.**

HANOI. — Air France, 41, rue Paul-Bert. Tel. : 820. Telegr. : AIRFRANS HANOI. - **Hotel Métropole.**

HONG-KONG. — Messageries Maritimes, 3 Ice House Street. Tel. : 26651. Telegr. : AIRFRANS HONG-KONG. **Peninsula Hotel.**

JASK. — Sayed Mohamed Saleh and Sons. Telegr. . SAYED JASK. - **Hotel : Sayed Rest House.**

JODHPUR. — Sanghi Brothers. Residency Road. Tel. : 31 (local 149). Telegr. SANGHI JODHPUR. - **State Hotel.**

KARACHI. — Volkart Brothers, Volkart Bldg. Mac Leod Road. Tel. : 2877. Telegr. : VOLKAIR KARACHI. - **Killarney Hotel.**

LONDON (Londres). — Air France, 52 Haymarket. Tel. : Whitehall 9671/74. Telegr. : AIRFRANS LESQUARE LONDON.

MARSEILLES. — Air France. 62, La Canebière. Tel. : Colbert 34-97. Telegr. : AIRFRANS MARSEILLES. Marignane Airport. Tel. : Colbert 81-94. - **Hotel de Noailles.**

NAPLES (Napoli). — Ala Littoria, Molo Beverello. Tel. : 25368. Telegr. : ALEREA NAPLES. - Air France, 265, Via Roma. Tel. : 20-671. Telegr. : AIRFRANS NAPLES. - **Hotel Excelsior.**

NEW YORK. — French Line (Cie Generale Transatlantique) 610 Fifth Avenue. Tel. : Columbus 5-2300. Telegr. : TRANSAT NEWYORK.

PARIS. — Air France, Central Booking Office, 2, rue Scribe. Tel. : Opera 41-00. Telegr. : AIRFRANSAG PARIS. Information Office, 2, rue Marbeuf.

RANGOON. — Du Bern, 140 Sule Pagoda Road. Tel. : Central 276 and 924. Telegr. : BERNICE-RANGOON. - **Minto Mansions Hotel.**

SAIGON. — Air France, 98, rue Catinat. Tel. : 21-608. Telegr. : AIRFRANS SAIGON. - **Hotel Continental.**

SHANGHAI. — Messageries Maritimes, 9, quai de France, P. O. B. 301. Telegr. : MESSAGERIES SHANGHAI.

TRIPOLI (SYRIA). — Air rrance, Tripoli. Tel. : 3-05. Telegr. : AIRFRANS TRIPOLI. - **Hakim Palace Hotel.**

14

PASSENGER FARES BAGGAGE AND FREIGHT RATES

The fares shown hereafter include meals and hotel accommodation en route, and transport to and from the town departure stations and the aerodromes.

FARES LIABLE TO ALTERATION WITHOUT PREVIOUS NOTICE.

DESTINATIONS	SINGLE	RETURN available 12 months	Excess baggage (a) and freight(b)
From AKYAB to :			£
ATHENS	70	126	7/-
BAGHDAD	40	72	4/-
BANGKOK	20	36	2/-
BASRA	40	72	4/-
BEIRUT	55	99	5/6
BUSHIRE	40	72	4/-
CASTELROSSO	60	108	6/-
CORFU	71	128	7/1
DAMASCUS	55	99	5/6
HANOI	35	63	3/6
HONG-KONG	40	72	4/-
JASK	27	49	2/8
LONDON	95	171	9/6
MARSEILLES	89	160	8/11
NAPLES	82	148	8/2
PARIS	65	108	6/-
SAIGON	30	54	3/-
TRIPOLI (Syria)	55	99	5/6
From ALLAHABAD to :			£
ATHENS	65	117	6/6
BAGHDAD	35	63	3/6
BANGKOK	30	54	3/-
BASRA	35	63	3/6
BEIRUT	50	90	5/-
BUSHIRE	26	47	2/7
CASTELROSSO	55	99	5/6
CORFU	66	119	6/7
DAMASCUS	50	90	5/-
HANOI	45	81	4/6
HONG-KONG	50	90	5/-
JASK	32	40	2/2
LONDON	90	162	9/-
MARSEILLES	84	151	8/5
NAPLES	77	139	7/8
PARIS	90	162	9/-
SAIGON	40	72	4/-
TRIPOLI (Syria)	56	101	5/7
From ATHENS to :			£
AKYAB	70	126	7/-
ALLAHABAD	65	117	6/6
BAGHDAD	38	68	3/10
BANGKOK	45	81	4/6
BASRA	43	77	4/4
BEIRUT	21	38	2/1
BUSHIRE	48	86	4/10
CALCUTTA	70	126	7/-
CASTELROSSO	10	18	1/-
CORFU	14	—	1/-
DAMASCUS	21	38	2/1
HANOI	105	189	10/6
HONG-KONG	110	198	11/-
JASK	56	101	5/7

DESTINATIONS	SINGLE	RETURN available 12 months	Excess baggage (a) and freight(b)
From ATHENS (contd) to :			£
JODHPUR	63	113	6/4
KARACHI	60	108	6/-
LONDON	32	58	3/2
MARSEILLES	23	41	2/4
NAPLES	15	27	1/6
PARIS	30	54	3/-
RANGOON	75	135	7/6
SAIGON	100	180	10/-
TRIPOLI (Syria)	21	38	2/1
From BAGHDAD to :			£
AKYAB	40	72	4/-
ALLAHABAD	35	63	3/6
ATHENS	38	68	3/10
BANGKOK	60	108	6/-
BASRA	6	11	-/7
BEIRUT	15	27	1/6
BUSHIRE	10	18	1/-
CALCUTTA	40	72	4/-
CASTELROSSO	27	49	2/8
CORFU	39	70	3/11
DAMASCUS	15	27	1/6
HANOI	75	135	7/6
HONG-KONG	80	144	8/-
JASK	22	40	2/2
JODHPUR	33	59	3/4
KARACHI	30	54	3/-
LONDON	62	112	6/2
MARSEILLES	55	99	5/6
PARIS	62	112	6/2
RANGOON	70	126	7/-
SAIGON	70	126	7/-
TRIPOLI (Syria)	15	27	1/6
From BANGKOK to :			£
AKYAB	20	36	2/-
ALLAHABAD	30	54	3/-
ATHENS	90	162	9/-
BAGHDAD	60	108	6/-
BASRA	60	108	6/-
BEIRUT	75	135	7/6
BUSHIRE	50	90	5/-
CALCUTTA	15	27	1/6
CASTELROSSO	80	144	8/-
CORFU	91	164	9/2
DAMASCUS	75	135	7/6
HANOI	20	36	2/-
HONG-KONG	25	45	2/6
JASK	47	85	4/8
JODHPUR	45	81	4/6
KARACHI	40	72	4/-
LONDON	115	207	11/6
MARSEILLES	109	196	10/11

DESTINATIONS	SINGLE	RETURN available 12 months	Excess baggage (a) and freight(b)
From BANGKOK (contd) to :			£
NAPLES	102	184	10/2
PARIS	115	207	11/6
RANGOON	15	27	1/6
SAIGON	15	27	1/6
TRIPOLI (Syria)	75	135	7/6
From BASRA to :			£
AKYAB	40	72	4/-
ALLAHABAD	35	63	3/6
ATHENS	43	77	4/4
BANGKOK	60	108	6/-
BEIRUT	21	38	2/1
BUSHIRE	6	11	-/7
CALCUTTA	40	72	4/-
CASTELROSSO	33	59	3/4
CORFU	44	79	4/5
DAMASCUS	21	38	2/1
HANOI	75	135	7/6
HONG-KONG	80	144	8/-
JASK	18	32	1/10
JODHPUR	33	59	3/4
KARACHI	28	50	2/10
LONDON	67	121	6/8
MARSEILLES	61	110	6/1
NAPLES	53	95	5/4
PARIS	45	81	4/6
RANGOON	70	126	7/-
SAIGON	70	126	7/-
TRIPOLI (Syria)	21	38	2/1
From BEIRUT			
TRIPOLI or DAMASCUS to :			Frs.
AKYAB	9.400	16.900	47. »
ALLAHABAD	8.000	14.400	40. »
ATHENS	3.000	5.400	15. »
BAGHDAD	2.000	3.600	10. »
BANGKOK	2.800	23.000	64. »
BASRA	3.700	6.700	14. »
BUSHIRE	4.100	7.400	20. »
CALCUTTA	9.400	16.900	47. »
CASTELROSSO	1.500	2.700	7.50
CORFU	3.200	5.800	16. »
HANOI	14.500	26.100	72.50
HONG-KONG	16.500	29.700	82.50
JASK	5.600	10.100	28. »
JODHPUR	7.400	13.300	37. »
KARACHI	7.000	12.600	35. »
LONDON	6.600	11.900	33. »
MARSEILLES	5.600	10.100	28. »
NAPLES	4.200	7.600	21. »
PARIS	7.000	12.600	35. »
RANGOON	12.000	21.600	60. »
BEYROUTH	—	—	—

DESTINATIONS	SINGLE	RETURN available 12 months	Excess baggage (a) and freight(b)
From CALCUTTA to :			£
ATHENS	70	126	7/-
BAGHDAD	40	72	4/-
BANGKOK	25	45	2/6
BASRA	40	72	4/-
BEIRUT	55	99	5/6
BUSHIRE	60	108	6/-
CASTELROSSO	71	128	7/1
DAMASCUS	55	99	5/6
HANOI	40	72	4/-
HONG-KONG	45	81	4/6
JASK	27	49	2/8
LONDON	95	171	9/6
MARSEILLES	89	160	8/11
NAPLES	82	148	8/2
PARIS	95	171	9/6
SAIGON	24	43	2/5
TRIPOLI (Syria)	55	99	5/6
From CORFU to :			£
AKYAB	71	128	7/1
ALLAHABAD	66	119	6/7
ATHENS	4	7	-/5
BAGHDAD	39	70	3/11
BANGKOK	91	164	9/1
BASRA	44	79	4/5
BEIRUT	24	43	2/5
BUSHIRE	49	88	4/11
CALCUTTA	71	128	7/1
CASTELROSSO	14	25	1/5
DAMASCUS	24	43	2/5
HANOI	106	191	10/7
HONG-KONG	111	200	11/1
JASK	57	103	5/8
JODHPUR	64	115	6/5
KARACHI	62	112	6/2
LONDON	29	52	2/11
MARSEILLES	20	36	2/-
NAPLES	11	19	1/2
PARIS	27	49	2/8
RANGOON	76	137	7/7
SAIGON	101	182	10/1
TRIPOLI (Syria)	24	43	2/5
From DAMASCUS			
See fares from Beirut.			
From HANOI to :			Frs.
AKYAB	5.100	9.200	25.50
ALLAHABAD	6.800	12.200	34. »
ATHENS	16.300	29.300	81.50
BAGHDAD	12.200	22.000	61. »
BANGKOK	3.000	5.400	15. »
BASRA	12.200	22.000	61. »
BEYROUTH	14.500	26.100	72.50

SUPPLEMENTARY SERVICE : DAMASCUS-BAGHDAD :

DAMASCUS-BAGHDAD single Frs. 1.800, 6 months return Frs. 2.900 BAGHDAD-DAMASCUS single £ 10.0.0, 6 months return £ 16.0.0
BEIRUT-BAGHDAD single Frs. 1.950, 6 months return Frs. 3.100 BAGHDAD-BEIRUT single £ 10.10.0, 6 months return £ 17.0.0

6

Two Air France Bloch 220s (F-AOHB *Gascogne* and F-AQNP *Alsace*) in company with a Lufthansa Focke Wulf Condor at London Croydon in 1938. The Bloch 220s entered service with Air France in 1937, sixteen examples being built. Some surviving examples were used post-war by Air France. (*GPJ Collection*)

Opening up the post-war route between France (Bicarrosse) and Fort de France, Martinique, in 1948, Air France flew three of the eight Latécoère Laté 631s built (c/ns 03, 04 and 06), six-engine seaplanes that could carry forty-six passengers. F-BDRA (c/n 04) is seen here during its first visit to Great Britain, the Solent at Southampton, in July 1947. The prototype first flew in March 1945. (*MJH*)

3

1940s
Air France at War

Although flying took place by Air France during WWII, it wasn't until 2 January 1946 that *Société Nationale Air France* came into existence and was charged by the French government with reviving the nation's civil air transport infrastructure.

1940s

THIS FOLLOWED FROM A JUNE 1945 MINISTERIAL DECISION FOR THE 'NATIONALISATION' OF FRANCE'S POST-WAR COMMERCIAL AIR TRANSPORT SERVICES. ALREADY THERE WAS AN AIR SERVICE FROM PARIS TO ALGERIA IN OPERATION AND, IN CONJUNCTION WITH THE AMERICANS, HUNDREDS OF FRENCH PRISONERS OF WAR WERE REPATRIATED IN 1945 BY A FLEET OF C-47S FLOWN FROM LOCATIONS IN GERMANY AND POLAND TO PARIS LE BOURGET.

Even after the September 1939 start of WWII and the initial occupation of parts of France, Air France services continued to North Africa, albeit that the whole French airline industry was now militarised. On 14 October 1939 a Lioré et Olivier LéO H.246 went into service on the Marseilles to Algiers route, replacing a LéO H.242. Air France flew this four-engine flying boat across the Mediterranean until November 1942 under the name of Service Civil de Liaisons Aériennes (SCLA). During the German occupation of southern France, three such aircraft were confiscated by the Germans and used to operate clandestine flights in support of German secret agents throughout Western Europe and North Africa. Two examples survived and after D-Day were recovered by Air France and reintroduced on the Marseilles to Algiers route.

SCLA had been created after the French 'armistice' in June 1940, under the auspices of the Armée de l'Air, led by Didier Daurat. The organisation was split into two, one serving metropolitan France and based in Marseilles and the other North Africa, based in Algiers. This latter operation flew Goéland and Caudron Simoun aircraft, transporting couriers and making humanitarian flights. Dewoitine 338s were also used, including the former *Ville de Bayrouth* renamed *Belfort* and registered in a unique and special sequence, FL-AQB (these identification marks were also used by Lignes Aériennes (LAM) aircraft); the former *Ville de Paris* was renamed *Verdun* (F-ARIE) and also flew with LAM. As well as flying services to Djibouti and Madagascar, one of the most important 'courier routes' linked Tunis, Algiers, Casablanca and Lisbon.

From 1941, Air France also started up again, but flying the 'Vichy Routes' on behalf of the Vichy French. This new manifestation of the Air France name replaced SCLA and

Dewoitine D.338 F-AQBG in the dual civil/military colours of Lignes Aériennes Militaires (LAM) operating at Damascus, Syria. This picture is probably taken immediately post-war because in the background a Junkers Ju-52 can be seen, Air France operating as many as sixty of this German-designed tri-motor aircraft between 1945 and 1954. (*JU*)

incorporated Air Afrique, Air Bleu, Air France Transatlantique and Aéromaritime. Dewoitine 342, three-engine, twenty-four passenger transports were used by this operation, primarily flying from France to Ameur el Ain in Algeria. They carried French civil registrations (F-ARIZ for example) but were distinguished by yellow stripes on the wings and a yellow vertical and horizontal tail surface, complemented by the blue, white and red national colours on the rudder.

It was also during the war that Réseau des Lignes Aériennes Françaises (RLAF) operated the Lignes Aériennes Militaires (LAM) throughout North and Equatorial Africa, having been established in Damascus, Syria, in 1941 by Lionel de Marmier (a former Air France test pilot) to provide air transport for the Free French territories. General Charles de Gaulle made extensive use of the LAM's quasi-military air operations as soon as they went into service. Lockheed L-18 (C-60A) 'Lodestar' aircraft were used for these services, wearing military roundels, the Air France logo on the nose and bearing civilian registrations – F-BAMJ, F-BAMK, F-BAML and F-BAMM were four of the ten different Lockheed 18s used between 1941 and 1948. Dewoitine 338s and Potez 62s were also used by LAM. The first LAM service flew on 14 November 1941 on a North African route.

On 22 December 1942, a route from Damascus to Tananarive (also known as Antananarivo) in Madagascar via Cairo, Wadi Halfa, Khartoum, Asmara, Djibouti, Mogadishu, Nairobi and Lindi was inaugurated with L-18 FL-AZM. By 1943 LAM's route network stretched from Algiers in the north, to Cairo, Khartoum, Accra and as far south as Madagascar. Flights were also made to Moscow via Tehran, Baku and Stalingrad. Men and equipment served the Allied cause, under the French government in North Africa, carrying hospital supplies and troops to the front line. Most of LAM's operations originated in Algiers, North Africa, because it was here in spring 1944 that the first provisional, new government of La République was being established in anticipation of the end of World War II. Max Hymans was installed as the first 'Director' of LAM.

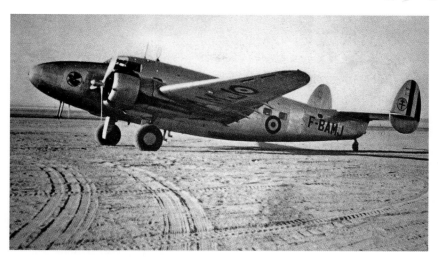

One of the ten Lockheed L-18s that operated with LAM and Air France between November 1941 and February 1948, wearing a mixture of civil and military colours. (*GPJ Collection*)

In 1944 all air transport entities, including LAM, were grouped into a military network divided into three distinct sections: the *Réseau Central* (RCTAM), the *Réseau Oriental* (ROTAM) and the *Réseau Atlantique* (RATAM). De Gaulle used a LAM Lockheed 18, wearing appropriate French military colours, to visit the French task force in Naples, Italy, operating alongside the British and Americans, in 1944. One of the main exponents of LAM and its later offshoots and also LAM's 'commandant', Lionel de Marmier, died in a tragic crash in December 1944. In the latter stages of the War, LAM aircraft started to adopt French civilian registrations and the traditional Air France 'hippocampe' or seahorse logo. On 1 July 1944, the LAM and Réseau Aérien Militaire Français (RAMF) were amalgamated to form Transports Aériens Militaires (TAM). During 1945 most of the remaining Lockheed L-18s were withdrawn, one of the last commercial flights they operated being on 23 July 1945 between Damascus and Beirut.

In 1946, Air France's Centre d'Exploitation d'Orly was opened and with Douglas DC-4s joining the fleet, arrangements were made to re-inaugurate scheduled services to New York, Rio de Janeiro, Buenos Aires, Brazzaville, Lagos, Saigon and Shanghai as quickly as possible. This last city rejoined the Air France network on 10 January 1947 when DC-4 F-BBDE arrived carrying the

Latécoère Laté 631 F-BANT *Lionel de Marmier* named after the founder of the Free French airline, LAM, pictured in February 1946. (*JU*)

new French ambassador for China. Lockheed 049 Constellations also joined Air France, the first (F-BAZC) arriving in Paris on 19 February 1947 and these US manufactured types were complemented by the indigenous SE.161 Languedoc, used by Air France for new European and Mediterranean services, including those to London's Croydon airport. Junkers Ju-52s were also used by Air France after the war, but mainly for air cargo/mail flights.

Services – initially mainly postal – to French protectorates, resumed even before the official end of World War II. On 4 February 1945, the first service was flown to Réunion in the Indian Ocean, initially from Algiers but soon from Le Bourget. Lockheed L-18s were used along with Junkers Ju-52s but by May 1947 this 'ligne Imperial' was flown from Paris using a Douglas DC-4, in a time of 49 hours with six intermediate stops. This compared to the four or five days taken by the Lockheed L-18 with fourteen intermediate stops. In 1947 there were daily Air France Lockheed flights from Algiers to Bône and to Oran, Rabat and Casablanca. Other services were flown from Algiers to Tunis four times a week, and

Algiers to Bône and Tunis weekly. The longest route was Algiers to Addis Ababa with eleven intermediate stops, flown bi-weekly and taking four days each way. The last recorded Air France Lockheed L-18 flights were flown in January and February 1948 on routes from Algiers to Bone, Algiers to Cairo via El Adem, Algiers to Casablanca via Oran and Rabat and finally from Tunis to Rome.

In August 1947, Air France re-established Laté 631 transatlantic flying boat services to the French West Indies, the Antilles. They had a fleet of nine of these six-engine, 70-ton pre-war designed types. They had a 188ft wing-span and could carry forty-six passengers, but the loss of one on a delivery flight and the forced landing of another in mid-Atlantic led to the Laté 631 being replaced by a Lockheed Constellation on these services. In 1950, three Laté 631s were sold to France Hydro to ferry cotton to the French Cameroons, an operation that lasted until September 1955.

In July 1947, Air France established the first local air services between the islands of the French Antilles using Catalina seaplanes, because land-based airports had not yet been established in Martinique and Guadeloupe. Three Catalinas were acquired, each equipped with twenty-two seats. These services ceased in 1950. This was the same year that Air France started Lockheed Constellation services from New York to Pointe-à-Pitre, a continuation of its Paris-New York service. With the establishment of land-based airports, Air France re-commenced services between Pointe-à-Pitre, Saint-Martin and Fort de France in 1952 using two Douglas DC-3s, followed in 1953 by a service from Fort de France to Cayenne in French Guiana.

In the South Pacific, Air France was also busy re-establishing air links between the far-flung and remote islands under French control. On 1 December 1948 the first Air France Saigon to Nouméa, New Caledonia, flight took place and on 27 September 1949, after a six-day flight,

a Douglas DC-4 realised the first post-war service from Paris to Nouméa; in 1950 this was extended from Nouméa to Bora Bora. A Catalina was used here as well for a short while, to extend the service on to Tahiti.

Post-war there was considerable rivalry between the state flag carrier, Air France, and two well-financed independent rivals, Union Aéromaritime de Transport (UAT), founded from Aéromaritime in 1949, and Transports Aériens Intercontinentaux (TAI); see Chapter 8 for more information. UAT's order for three DH Comet 1As prompted Air France's rival order, all three delivered in July 1953. TAI took over most of the air services established by Air France in the South Pacific during the 1950s.

Bloch 220s first entered service with Air France in 1937. Aircraft that survived WWII helped Air France establish its first post-war services, including this example named *Edouard Serre*, pictured in 1946. Bloch 220s were eventually retired from service in 1949 as more DC-3s were acquired. (*GPJ Collection*)

Bloch 220 F-AOHC (c/n 3), still in basic French
military colours, at London Croydon airport
in 1946 operating early post-war Air France
flights, in company with DC-3/C-47s
of other European nationalities. (*MJH*)

Postale de Nuit

THE POSTALE DE NUIT – UNDER THIS NAME – WAS FOUNDED IN 1945 UNDER THE DIRECTION OF DIDIER DAURAT AND RAYMOND VANIER, INITIALLY AT LE BOURGET, BUT LATER AT THE CENTRE D'EXPLOITATION POSTALE AT PARIS ORLY AIRPORT. A FLEET OF JUNKERS JU 52S WERE USED INITIALLY BUT BY 1948 HAD BEEN ENTIRELY REPLACED BY FIFTEEN DC-3S. SIX DC-4S JOINED THE POSTALE DE NUIT OPERATION IN 1961 WHEN RETIRED FROM PASSENGER DUTIES.

Almost as soon as Air France became operational again after WWII, the inauguration of the Postale de Nuit became a priority: the first Air France flight on 26 October 1945 was a Postale de Nuit service from Paris to Bordeaux, Toulouse and Pau. Douglas DC-3s that had flown with passengers during the day, were commandeered, had their seats removed and operated these night-time duties based on Paris Le Bourget. F-BCYV was one of the many DC-3s used, to be complemented in the late 1950s and 1960s by Douglas DC-4s retired from all passenger duties by 1961.

In the mid-1950s, the Postale de Nuit service was flying as many as 5,980 night landings a year, including 130 'instrument landings' and maintaining a 98% on-time performance. They soon coined the name *hiboux* or 'night owls' for the crews. The first of a dedicated fleet of Fokker F.27 Friendship freighters was delivered in September 1968. By 1981 Air France's Postale de Nuit was operating a fleet of fifteen Fokker F.27-500 Friendships and four Nord C-160P Transall dedicated freighters, supplied to them by France's Postal Administration. The F.27s could carry 5.86 tonnes of mail and the Transalls 14.2 tonnes, carried in twenty-four special containers. Based at small and large regional airports from Bastia (Corsica) in the south, to Brest (Brittany) in the north-west, these aircraft flew to the nation's postal 'hub' at Paris Orly six nights a week. The Transalls, replacements for

Caudron C.440 *Goéland* of Cie Air Transport, similar to the aircraft used by Air Bleu and then Air France to inaugurate Air France's night mail service on 10 May 1939. This picture was taken at Croydon, London, in August 1946. (*MJH*)

DC-4s, were in service between 1973 and 1992, and mainly used for freight/mail to and from the French Mediterranean island of Corsica.

Flying French mail, particularly internationally, by air had been the *raison d'être* for many of the pioneering French airlines prior to the 1933 formation of Air France, and subsequently remained an important aim of French aviation. As in the US, the mail came before passengers as a driving force in the founding of many scheduled air services. Compagnie Générale Aéropostale quickly became famous for flying the nation's mail to overseas territories in northern and western Africa, from April 1927 onwards, followed in 1930 by its pioneering South American services to Brazil and Chile with Jean Mermoz. The airline's name, however, disappeared when it merged into Air Union and then Air France in 1933.

L'Aéropostale re-emerged in 1990 as Inter Ciel Service (ICS), which had been launched on 13 January 1987 as Inter Cargo System, in order to accelerate postal deliveries following the introduction of La Poste's new *Chronoposte* product. The service was formed by integrating TAT Express (see Chapter 9) and La Poste's Boeing 737-200C convertibles to form a new French cargo and passenger airline. ICS was a joint venture between Air Inter, Air France, TAT and Sofipost, but previously had been operating Vickers Vanguard Merchantman (on lease from Europe Aéro Service of Perpignan) and a Lockheed C-130 Hercules (F-GFZE).

The Fokker F.27-500s, which were being operated by Air France on behalf of La Poste, the French mail services, had been in operation since 1968/69. They were phased out of service during the 1990s, replaced by a rationalised network of L'Aéropostale Boeing 737s, which were, in fact, modified former Aéromaritime/UTA passenger Boeing 737-300s. The number of out-stations was also reduced to ten, but with fifty flights flown between these ten cities. The last four F.27s operated on the nights of 14 and 15 January 2000 to and from Toulouse at the end of 55 years of 'La Ronde de Nuit de la Postale'.

Above: Joining the Air France fleet in 1948, the Douglas C-47A DC-3 conversion F-BCYV was one of the first aircraft used by Air France to resume its Postale de Nuit service operated from Le Bourget. (*GPJ Collection*)

Above: SNCASE SE.161 Languedoc F-BATD in November 1946. (*JU*)

Left: 1947 saw the widespread introduction of the SNCASE SE.161 Languedoc to general European cities services with Air France. Pictured is F-BATD (No4), its four 1,020hp Gnome-Rhône engines at full power. The type was introduced on North African services in 1946, notably Paris to Algiers and Casablanca, where F-BATJ also served. (*GPJ Collection*)

Left: Three ex-British European Airways (BEA) DH.89 Dragon Rapide aircraft were sold to Air France and exported from the UK to Le Bourget on 21 April 1948. F-BEDX, F-BEDY and F-BEDZ were swiftly moved to Air France outposts in Madagascar and Algeria. (*MJH*)

1940s

Opening up the post-war route between France (Bicarrosse) and Fort de France, Martinique, in 1948, Air France flew three of the eight Latécoère Laté 631s built (c/ns 03, 04 and 06), six-engine seaplanes that could carry forty-six passengers. F-BDRA (c/n 04) is seen here during its first visit to Great Britain, the Solent at Southampton, in July 1947. The prototype first flew in March 1945. (MJH)

Right: Lockheed L-049 Constellation F-BAZB (c/n 2073) on a pre-delivery flight from Lockheed's Burbank, California, works in the latter part of 1946; it was delivered to Air France on 4 December. (*GPJ Collection/ Musée de l'Air*)

Left: Taking over from Douglas DC-4s, Air France's Lockheed L-749A Constellation fleet started to serve transatlantic routes. F-BAZL, delivered in August 1947, is seen here crossing the freeway taxiway bridge at New York's Idlewild airport. (*GPJ Collection*)

Right: Air France took delivery of this Lockheed L-749A Constellation F-BAZL (c/n 2538) in August 1947. The aircraft's last user was the Senegal government and it was scrapped at Toussus-le-Noble in 1979 after an illustrious career with the national airline. (*Peter Keating Collection*)

Air France Cargo

C ARRIAGE OF CARGO IS AN IMPORTANT FACET OF ANY AIRLINE BUSINESS, HISTORICALLY AND IN CONTEMPORARY OPERATIONS. WHILST AIR FRANCE'S PRE-WAR HISTORY – PARTICULARLY WITH AIR MAIL FLIGHTS (SEE CHAPTER 2) – INVOLVED CARRIAGE OF CARGO, IT WAS NOT UNTIL THE 1950S THAT DEDICATED AIR CARGO AIRCRAFT BECAME AN IMPORTANT PART OF THE AIRLINE'S OPERATION. BETWEEN 1953 AND 1956, AIR FRANCE'S CARGO BUSINESS GREW FROM 48 TO 74 THOUSAND TONNES/KILOMETRES, AND THE 1956 CARGO TOTAL REPRESENTED A 21% INCREASE OVER 1955'S TOTAL. MOST OF THIS GROWTH WAS ON AIR FRANCE'S INTERNATIONAL ROUTES.

The gargantuan – for the time – Bréguet 763 'Deux Ponts' exemplified the role that cargo played in Air France's post-war history, as shown by the historic order for twelve placed by Max Hymans in 1952. These aircraft could carry forty tons of cargo. These were 'combi' aircraft (passengers and cargo) but in 1965 they became dedicated freighters for Air France.

The last commercial Air France 'Deux Ponts' flight was flown by F-BASN on 31 March 1971.

Air France was the first customer for the Boeing 707-320, with twenty 707-328s being delivered from 1960 to 1962. With the experience gained using the 707 on intercontinental passenger services, a specialist cargo branch was established between 1967 and 1968 with the addition of seven Boeing 707-328C 'combi' aircraft (convertible passenger/cargo variant), which were christened 'Pélican' – the Pélican logo was worn on the nose of the aircraft, and also on the inside of the large forward cargo door, so that when loading was in progress and the door opened upwards the logo and words 'Cargo Jet Le Pélican' could be seen. The increasing volume of air cargo carried by Air France is illustrated by the comparison of the 1959 and 1969 figures, an increase from 73,000 to 338,000 tonne kilometres.

Air France's first all-passenger Boeing 747 was delivered on 9 March 1970. Later Air France ordered ten 'Super Pélican' Boeing 747-200F freighters (with Pratt & Whitney JTD9D-7 engines), the first being delivered in late 1974, but it was another two years before the second aircraft arrived: F-BPVR, this time with CF6-50E engines instead. The Boeing 747-228Fs of Air France carried a 94 tonne payload on a typical long haul flight. By the mid-1990s, Air France's total Boeing 747 fleet had increased to forty-five aircraft, of which ten were

With their special nose door, Air France Cargo's Boeing 747-200 freighters were in extensive use for transporting outsize cargo including this CFM International engine. (*GPJ Collection*)

The order for twelve French-built Deux Ponts transports propelled Air France into mainstream air cargo operations. Their versatility is demonstrated here in the heat of the North African desert in Algeria. (*JU*)

wholly dedicated freighters and seventeen the 'combi' versions, designated SCDs. The aircraft wore a small 'Super Pélican' logo between the fuselage Air France title and the word 'cargo'.

Following the Air France-KLM merger in 2004, the cargo activities of both airlines were consolidated. By October 2005 Air France Cargo and KLM Cargo had formally merged, with a Joint Cargo Management Team operating the organisation worldwide from a base in the Netherlands. In 2007 President and Chief Operating Officer Pierre-Henri Gourgeon announced that the phasing out of Air France Cargo's 'Super Pélican' Boeing 747-200F 'classics' would be accelerated as the Air France-KLM Group decided to scale back its cargo fleet wholesale. The Group considered that it had air cargo overcapacity, a nine-month period in 2006 seeing a 41.3% decline in income from the same period in 2005. By the end of 2007 all of its uneconomic, fuel-guzzling Boeing 747-200s, both cargo and passenger versions, were phased out of service, about 15 months ahead of their original retirement schedule.

This is part of a wholesale attempt by Air France-KLM to reduce costs and increase efficiency. In mid-2007 Air France Cargo took delivery of the first of three Boeing 747BCFs (Boeing Converted Freighters) to replace its 747-200Fs. Taikoo Aircraft Engineering in Xiamen in China undertook the conversion work from Boeing 747-400 Combis and the remaining two 747BCFs were delivered before the end of 2007.

In June 2007, in a further move to rationalise the Air France-KLM cargo business while expanding geographically, the European airline began exclusive talks with China Southern Airlines to establish a Chinese cargo joint venture. The two airlines signed a preliminary agreement on 28 June, aimed at China Southern joining the SkyTeam alliance (see Chapter 10) in due course.

Sud Aviation SE.210 Caravelle III F-WHRA, the second Caravelle delivered to Air France (F-BHRB was the first on 19 March 1959) during its first flight on 18 May 1958. (*JU*)

4

1950s
The World's Largest Airline

Max Hymans, who had been inspirational in the post-war revival of Air France, became the airline's President in July 1948, and was to be the driving force behind the incredible growth of the airline during the 1950s. He retired as President in January 1961. It was under his leadership, with Henri Ziegler as Director General, that major fleet orders were placed for some of the world's most revolutionary new airliner types.

1950s

U NDER HENRI ZIEGLER'S REIGN, AIR FRANCE BECOME 'THE WORLD'S LARGEST AIRLINE', A REMARKABLE FEAT SO SOON AFTER THE END OF WWII. IN 1956 AN AIR FRANCE AIRCRAFT TOOK OFF OR LANDED SOMEWHERE IN THE WORLD EVERY 3.5 MINUTES AND BY 1957 AIR FRANCE SERVED 236 CITIES IN 73 COUNTRIES. IN THE FIVE YEARS BETWEEN 1952 AND 1957 IT CARRIED 8 MILLION PASSENGERS, AND IN THE TEN YEARS AFTER THE COMMENCEMENT OF TRANSATLANTIC SERVICES TO THE US, IT HAD CARRIED 350,000 PASSENGERS. BETWEEN 1949 AND 1957 THE AIRLINE'S REVENUE TRIPLED.

Air France was one of four airlines to establish IATA, the International Air Transport Association. IATA was fundamental in establishing many things that are taken for granted today: basic international commercial documents, bills of landing and even passenger tickets. And despite being a nationalised airline, Air France also advocated

freedom of the skies and competition, modelling itself on some of the burgeoning US airlines of the time.

What today are called 'fifth freedom rights' (the right of airlines from any two nations to collect passengers from each other's territory for transport to a destination in another country) were first used by Air France from the small 'hub' it had first established in New York International Airport (Idlewild) in July 1948. Following this a New York-Montreal-Paris service commenced in October 1950 and

Air France's globe-spanning network in 1952.(*AFM*)

Paris-New York-Mexico City in April 1952. On the
'Mid-Atlantic' system a new Paris-Caracas-Bogota service
started in January 1953, followed by Chicago-Montreal-
Paris in October.

Air France's 'tourist class' was introduced on the North
Atlantic on 1 May 1952, expanding the range of passenger
options that was now available. At the other end of the
scale it was also the time of the new super-luxury concept,
Golden Parisian (19 November 1953), possible with the
introduction of the first of ten Super Constellations,
which became Air France's flagship. In 1953 the Super
Constellations were followed by three de Havilland Comet
1As. Twelve Bréguet 763 'Deux Pont' or 'Provence'
passenger transports were ordered in 1952, mainly for
North African services and then in 1953 and 1954 orders
for twelve turbo-prop Vickers V.708 Viscounts. When the
problems with the Comet manifested themselves, and the
type was grounded early in 1954, the Boeing salesmen
were quick to knock on Hymans' Paris door and on
3 February 1956 Air France ordered ten examples
(soon to increase to seventeen) of the new Boeing 707 jet.

Like many of the world's major airlines the 'carrot' of
commercial jet travel was dangling close but not close
enough. Some airlines purchased pressurised Douglas

Lockheed L1049 Super Constellation F-BHBB long-range version
with tip-tanks in pre-delivery pictures in 1955. (*JU*)

DC-7s for their inter-continental routes, but Air France
chose to stay with Lockheed and ordered ten examples of
the Lockheed 1649 'Super Starliner'. TWA was the type's
main customer, with an order for twenty-four. Air France
initially ordered twelve examples, but reduced this to ten.
The first aircraft (F-BHBK) was delivered from Lockheed's
Burbank, California, works on 8 July 1957, flying non-stop
to Paris Orly in 17 hours and 11 minutes. Air France started
with a weekly *Golden Parisian* luxury service to New York
with seating for just thirty-two passengers but later with a
mixed configuration of sixteen first class and forty-nine
economy seats plus four 'berths'. Super Starliners were
also used for services from Paris to Montreal and Chicago.
The type's obsolescence was already imminent, and they
remained in service only until 1963, ousted by the arrival
of Boeing 707s. All survivors, except one exported to Africa
and one used by the Orly fire department, were scrapped
at Paris Orly in 1967.

The advent of aircraft such as the Super Constellation
and Super Starliner enabled Air France to develop a level
of in-flight service that many regarded as the best in the

world: 'A gourmet repast in a continental atmosphere' was how one writer described the Air France in-flight experience. Fine wines and master chefs, together with Limoges porcelain, Baccarat crystal glass and Christofle silver cutlery were what First Class customers came to expect on long inter-continental flights. Private sleeping compartments or 'Sky-Rooms' were also available on some aircraft and flights as part of the *Golden Parisian* service.

However, it was France's home-grown jet, the Sud SE.210 Caravelle with its Comet-style nose, that really confirmed the foresight and tenacity with which Hymans undertook his role of developing 'his' national airline. The prototype Caravelle (F-WHHH) first flew at Toulouse Blagnac on 27 May 1955 with Pierre Nadot as chief pilot. On 16 November 1955, Hymans announced that the French flag carrier would order twelve Caravelles, three for service entry late in 1958, six for 1959 and three for 1960. The contract between Air France and Sud Aviation was signed on the same day in February 1956 as the Boeing 707 order. The prototype Caravelle was rolled out in Air France colours on 12 May 1956, but it wasn't until 6 May 1959 that Air France inaugurated commercial passenger services with the Caravelle (F-BHRA *Alsace*) flying between Paris Orly and Rome (Ciampino), then on to Athens and Istanbul. The Caravelle replaced Lockheed 1049G Super Constellations. Soon after, on 1 June, Air France Caravelles replaced Vickers Viscounts on the Rome-Orly-Rome-Nice-Rome schedule and then on 27 July

replacing a TAI (chartered) DC-6 on the Paris-London (Heathrow)-Nice-London-Paris service.

Air France had established three maintenance bases by the end of the 1950s. Most important was the Orly Maintenance Centre, whose central hangar had a frontal opening of 162m (531ft) and a floor area of 7,678m^2 (9178 sq yds) and could accommodate four Super Constellations simultaneously. The other two were the Courbevoie Maintenance Centre which specialised in engine overhaul, and the Toulouse Maintenance Centre where all Douglas DC-3 and DC-4 maintenance was carried out.

At the end of the 1950s, Air France was carrying 2.78 million passengers per annum (1959 figure). Its fleet numbered 131 aircraft as follows, just prior to the delivery of the first Caravelle:

Lockheed 1649 Super Starliner	10
Lockheed 1049 Super Constellation	22
Lockheed 749 Constellation	15
Vickers V.708 Viscount	12
Bréguet 763 'Deux Ponts' or 'Provence'	12
Douglas DC-4	23
Douglas DC-3	37

The end of the 1950s and beginning of the 1960s was a further period of major expansion, when the capacity of Air France's fleet all but doubled.

Lockheed L-1649A-98-11 'Super Starliner' F-BHBL *Rochambeau* was delivered to Air France at Orly in July 1957, and was used on the airline's schedules to Chicago, Moscow, Mauritius and Tokyo (via Anchorage, Alaska). It operated for only six years, was stored for four at Orly and broken up there in 1967. (*GPJ Collection*)

Left: One of three DH Comet 1As that were acquired by Air France following wrangling between Overseas National Airways (ONA), the original customer for these aircraft, and the Civil Aeronautics Authority in the US over certification approval for the type. Air France eagerly put them into service on the Paris-Rome-Beirut schedule on 26 Aug 1953, as rival UAT/Aéromaritime had inaugurated Comet 1A jet service 19 February. F-BGNX, F-BGNY and F-BGNZ were the three aircraft used on Air France services to Casablanca, Algiers, Cairo until the 1954 Comet disasters caused the grounding of the type. (*GPJ Collection*)

Below: Vickers V.708 Viscount F-BGNR (c/n 35), one of a batch of twelve ordered in 1952 for service entry in 1953. Many of these aircraft were transferred to Air Inter's fleet (see Chapter 8). (*MJH*)

Right: Bréguet Deux Pont 763 F-BASV, one of twelve in the Air France fleet. They were mainly used on the airline's Mediterranean network as well as on Algerian domestic routes, but had all been retired from service by 1971. This example is pictured at Le Bourget in 1967 and was scrapped a couple of years later at Toulouse. (MJH)

Below: Stunning line-up of five Air France Lockheed Constellations at Paris Orly in late 1959: F-BAZH (c/n 2627) L-749A-79-46 nearest, delivered in February 1950, F-BHMJ (c/n 4669) a larger L-1049G-82-98 Super Constellation delivered December 1956 beyond. (*MJH*)

Above: Second prototype Sud Caravelle (c/n 02) F-BHHI (note the Sud Aviation logo on the tail) in the US
in mid-1957 on its extensive sales tour there. This aircraft was leased to Air France – and SAS – in 1958
and although subsequently used as a development and test aircraft it was withdrawn from use in 1969
and donated to the Air France (CIV) Centre d'Instruction de Vilgénis. (*JU*)

Below: Pontoise-Cormeilles-en-Vexin on the north-western outskirts of Paris was the base in the 1950s for the
Air France Pilot Training School, its 110 pilot instructors and mechanics and its large fleet (twenty-four aircraft)
of North American AT-6D Texans. F-BJBV is pictured. (*MJH*)

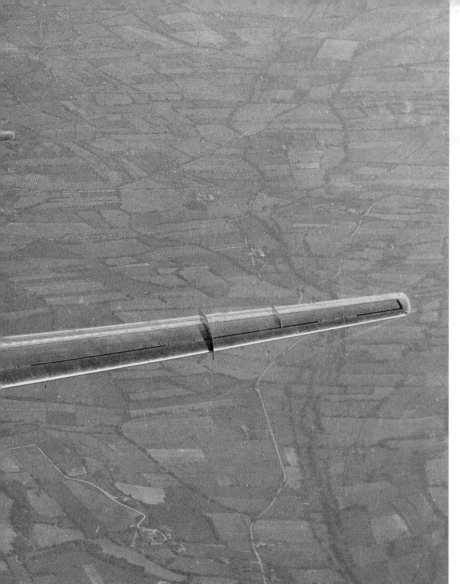

Opposite bottom and left:
Sud Aviation SE.210 Caravelle III
F-WHRA, the second Caravelle delivered
to Air France (F-BHRB was the first on
19 March 1959) during its first flight on
18 May 1958. (*JU*)

Below: The first Boeing 707-328 for
Air France, F-BHSA (c/n 17613)
Château de Versailles flew for the first time
on 11 September 1959, shown here
pre-delivery at Seattle. Air France took
delivery of this aircraft on 6 November
1959 and it entered service on the
Paris-New York route on 31 January 1960.
The last Air France Boeing 707 schedule
was flown on 28 October 1982.
(*GPJ Collection*)

The airline's clientele expected an 'experience' when flying Air France; naturally, smartly turned out flight attendants/stewardesses and pilots wearing up-to-the-minute fashions from the best of French fashion designers was a major part of the airline's image. Air Inter and UTA also realised the importance of making such a statement in dressing their air crews.

The fashionable outfitting of pilots and stewards (they weren't called flight attendants or air hostesses initially) was initiated almost immediately, with Lucien Boudet appointed as an Air France steward in 1934 aboard the airline's Wibault 283 T-12 tri-motors, a type derived from the Wibault 280, 281 and 282 used by predecessors CIDNA and Air Union. A 1930s Wibault crew comprised the chief pilot (captain), co-pilot and a steward, serving the ten passengers. For winter operations, the steward was attired in an extremely smart and formal uniform with dark jacket, waistcoat and high-neck shirt with bow tie. Thermos-type flasks were used for storing the in-flight hot drinks served to passengers, the Air

MAIN FRENCH AIRLINE UNIFORM DESIGNERS 1946-1969		
1946	Georgette Raynal	*for Air France*
1951	Georgette de Trezes	*for Air France*
1962	Marc Bohan at Christian Dior	*for Air France*
1964	Nina Ricci	*for UTA*
1968	Pierre Cardin	*for UTA*
1969	Cristóbal Balenciaga	*for Air France*

A 1951 uniform, designed by Georgette de Trezes, seen here alongside a Vickers Viscount, so presumably around 1953 after the delivery of the first Viscounts to Air France. (*AFM*)

France Wibaults being used mainly on services to European cities. Come summer the dark jacket changed to a white high-neck and the bow tie was discarded.

In 1946, couturière Georgette Raynal was chosen by Air France to design its air hostess uniforms. In the same year, the first intake of twenty-seven aspiring young ladies was assembled at Châteaux de Montjean for evaluation, selection and initial training, a rigorous procedure that included assessment of the girls' gymnastic ability! Raynal was retained to design the revised uniforms in 1948, and these now included the flight-deck crew for the first time, breaking away from the more formal, military-style uniforms of the immediate post-war era. During the 1950s Georgette de Trezes was the favoured designer, followed in the early 1960s by Dior. In 1969 Balenciaga was chosen as hemlines crept above

Above: Not to be outdone by its international rival, Air Inter ensured its crews were equally smart. This 1962 Air Inter Viscount crew are pictured before the first direct service between Nîmes and Clermont-Ferrand with (from left) Captain Paul Larribière, Jean Harbion, unknown and cabin chief Sissi Grosso. The photogenic Grosso appeared in numerous Air Inter publicity photos during the 1960s. (*GPJ Collection*)

Left: Fifteen crew ready to board an Air France intercontinental Boeing 707 flight – these uniforms were designed by Christian Dior in 1963. (*AFM*)

the knee. It became fair game for Paris couturiers to offer the national airline their wares; Nina Ricci, Carven, Louis Féraud, and even French artists such as Florent Margaritis were all involved in work depicting the airline and its staff.

Several epoch-making decisions by Air France's management were made during the 1960s – doubtless to increase the airline's public appeal and perception. In 1963, Air France air hostesses were allowed to be married for the first time and in 1968 the upper age limit of fifty years for female air hostesses was introduced.

Left: Most large airlines in Europe and North America chose different uniforms for their crews depending on the season – this is the Christian Dior-designed winter uniform introduced in late 1963. (*AFM*)

Above: With hemlines climbing, Balenciaga was chosen to design new uniforms for 1969.
Right: A hostess poses in front of those characteristically shaped windows of a Caravelle. (*AFM*)

The first Boeing 727-200 'Super B' for Air France, F-BOJA, was delivered to Paris Orly on 24 March 1968. (*MJH*)

5

1960s
The Jet Era

The start of the decade saw the formal opening of the new terminal building at Paris Orly 'Sud' in 1961. This became almost exclusively Air France 'territory', enabling the airline to improve customer service and efficiency.

1960s

AIR FRANCE'S INITIAL ORDER FOR NINE BOEING 727-228 TRI-JETS CONTINUED THE MOVE AWAY FROM THE USE OF DOMESTICALLY BUILT AIRLINERS; AIR FRANCE WAS ALREADY FLYING BOEING 707S AND VISCOUNTS. AIR FRANCE'S ORDER ALSO CAME FAIRLY LATE IN THE PRODUCTION SCHEDULE FOR 727S, WHICH HAD COMMENCED IN 1966 WITH DELIVERIES TO PAN AM. F-BOJA, THE FIRST 162-PASSENGER BOEING 727-200 'SUPER B' FOR AIR FRANCE WAS DELIVERED ON 24 MARCH 1968. ON 16 APRIL, AIR FRANCE'S FIRST BOEING 727 SERVICE WAS INAUGURATED BETWEEN PARIS AND LONDON HEATHROW AND BY 1969 THE AIRLINE HAD SIX OF THE TYPE IN SERVICE. A FURTHER TWENTY BOEING 727S WERE SUBSEQUENTLY ORDERED AND PLACED INTO SERVICE, F-GCDI THE LAST IN 1981.

On 7 February 1966, Air Charter International (ACI) – Société Aérienne Française d'Affretement – was formed as a wholly owned subsidiary of Air France in order to operate charter and inclusive tour services on behalf of the parent. Air Inter also had a stake in ACI. Initially Air France aircraft were used – Caravelles – but by 1978 ACI had obtained its own fleet, coincidentally with the same equipment, plus Boeing 727s. ACI's colour scheme also closely resembled that of its parent and aircraft even sported the name

'Air France', in the case of Caravelles, on the engine nacelles – the individual aircraft names from the days in the Air France fleet were also retained.

Air France was instrumental in the formation of the ATLAS alliance of major European airlines, the official protocol being signed by representatives of Air France,

SE.210 Caravelle III *Bourbonnais* F-BKGZ pictured in early 1962. (*JU*)

Boeing 707-328B F-BLCD *Chateau de Dampierre* was delivered to Air France in February 1966; subsequently painted in the airline's revised livery it was one of the last 707s retired from service and was presented for preservation to the Musée de l'Air at Le Bourget in 1984; see also 6.13. (*GPJ*)

Alitalia, Lufthansa and Sabena on 14 March 1969. ATLAS was primarily aimed at purchasing power and commonality in airliners and spares/engineering. It was established in competition to the KSSU alliance that had been formed in 1967 by rival national airlines KLM, Swissair and SAS, joined in 1970 by UTA (see Chapter 8). ATLAS erred in favour of Boeing and KSSU in favour of McDonnell Douglas for its forthcoming 'wide body' orders.

The 1960s was the 'jet era' for Air France as its Boeing 707s firmly established the company's international dominance. New York, Los Angeles and Rio de Janeiro were its most lucrative routes. With its 707s it also inaugurated the Paris to Tokyo route (via a southern routeing) on 12 January 1962. With the 1962 merger of UTA and TAI, Air France was able to take over some of TAI's former routes such as Paris-Dakar. Air France also pioneered the 'in-flight movie' in the 1960s on some of its long haul flights. Between 1963 and 1970 Air France's international traffic grew significantly and by 1966 exceeded 90% of its total. Overall traffic was growing at a rate of 7.5% per annum, an unprecedented figure, and in 1967, Air France was serving ninety-eight foreign cities direct from Paris.

By 1969, Air France was carrying 5.66 million passengers a year, an increase of almost 100% over its 1959 total. In 1965, Air France established its registered office in the Maine-Montparnasse district of Paris.

The international growth coincided with the 1966 announcement in Seattle of Boeing's launch of its 707 successor, the Boeing 747 or 'jumbo jet' wide body. The dilemma of which 'wide body' to order (the Douglas DC-10 and Lockheed L1011 Tristar were the rivals) was determined by Air France's membership of the ATLAS group, with the other member airlines deciding initially on orders for the Boeing 747 in 1969. Air France and other ATLAS member airlines were undoubtedly influenced by the need to compete with US airline Pan American, who had placed a launch order for 25 of the new transatlantic behemoths.

1960s

Right: SE.210 Caravelle III F-BHRZ *Flandre* at Paris Orly in June 1967, with another Caravelle beyond. This aircraft went to Air Inter in March 1971 and was withdrawn from use in December 1980. (*MJH*)

Below: 'Caravelle Country', with five Air France examples on a wet Paris Orly ramp in June 1967 with an interloping Pakistan International Airways Boeing 720-040. F-BHRS Caravelle III *Normandie* is nearest. (*MJH*)

Above: Air Charter International SE.210 Caravelle III F-BJTJ *Bourbonnais*, one of the first four aircraft transferred by Air France to the ACI fleet and shown at Cardiff's Rhoose airport in March 1976. (*GPJ*)

Left: Operating an Air France flight at London Heathrow in July 1974, ACI SE.210 Caravelle III F-BJTH. Another Caravelle, this one in Air France livery, can be seen in the distance. (*AIC*)

Right: Convair CV-990-30A-5 N5605 (c/n 9) was delivered to American Airlines in July 1962. In 1967 and 1968 it was leased to Air France by Modern Air Transport, its registered owner at the time. It is seen here at London Heathrow in April 1967. (*AIC*)

Below: As well as Cambrian's Viscount G-AMOC, Air France also leased British Eagle V.739 Viscount G-ATDU, seen here at Liverpool Speke in June 1968. (GM)

Opposite: This late-1960s Paris Orly shot provides an interesting comparison between the two main tri-jets of the 1960s. In the foreground is BEA HS.121 Trident Three G-AWZC, with Air France Boeing 727-228 F-BPJJ taxiing past. Another Air France 727-228, F-BOJB, is parked as well as a Middle East Airlines Boeing 707-3B4C, OD-AFD. (*MJH*)

One of Air France's fleet of Concordes. (*Aviation-Images.com*)

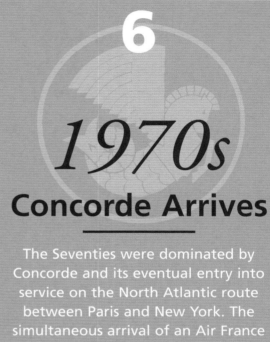

6

1970s

Concorde Arrives

The Seventies were dominated by Concorde and its eventual entry into service on the North Atlantic route between Paris and New York. The simultaneous arrival of an Air France Concorde and a British Airways Concorde (flown from London Heathrow) at New York's JFK international airport on 22 November 1977 was the result of years of political wrangling and delicate negotiations. It was also a masterpiece of organisation.

1970s

THE 1970S ALSO SAW AIR FRANCE — AND UTA — INSTALLED AT THE NEW TERMINAL ONE AT PARIS'S PRESTIGIOUS NEW AIRPORT, ROISSY-CHARLES DE GAULLE AIRPORT. THIS FUTURISTIC DEVELOPMENT OF A CENTRAL, CIRCULAR TERMINAL ACCESSIBLE TO SEVEN SUB-SATELLITES BY TUNNELS BENEATH THE INTERVENING TAXIWAY, SPELT OUT THE 'NEW FRANCE' AND THE 'NEW' AIR FRANCE WHICH TOOK UP RESIDENCE AT CHARLES DE GAULLE IN 1974. AIR FRANCE TRANSFERRED THE MAJORITY OF ITS FREIGHT OPERATIONS TO THE NEW AIRPORT FROM ORLY. ON THE OPPOSITE SIDE OF PARIS AT ORLY, AÉROPORTS DE PARIS (THE OPERATOR OF BOTH AIRPORTS, PLUS SEVERAL OTHER SMALLER PARIS AIRPORTS INCLUDING LE BOURGET) OPENED THE NEW ORLY-OUEST (ORLY-WEST) TERMINAL, BECOMING THE MAIN TERMINAL FOR AIR INTER, WHILST AIR FRANCE OCCUPIED ORLY-SUD (ORLY-SOUTH).

A crisis of economics was also a hallmark of the 1970s for Air France and many other airlines. Fare wars, the growth of the charter market with cheap all-inclusive packages and overcapacity were all characteristics of the decade, extending through to the 1980s as well. Air France's first scheduled Concorde flight to the US was to Washington-Dulles International on 23 May 1976, a joint Air France/British Airways extravaganza, a precursor of the joint Concorde arrival in New York's JFK over a year later. Before this though there were many Concorde route-proving and promotional flights – in 1971 Concorde flew from Paris to Dakar (Senegal, West Africa) and on to South America, the same year that the prototype Concorde flew to the Azores with President Pompidou on board for a meeting with US President Richard Nixon. A tour of Asia and Australasia followed in 1972, including visits to Tokyo and Australia. An Air France Concorde visited Dallas, Texas, on 23 September 1973 for the opening of the new Dallas-Fort Worth airport and then Fairbanks, Alaska, in February 1974 on cold-weather trials. Between 27 May and 5 June 1974 route-proving flights from Paris to Dakar and on to Rio de Janeiro made history on the route pioneered by Air France and Jean Mermoz several decades earlier. A trial transatlantic flight to Boston (Logan) airport on 17 June illustrated the time saving that passengers aboard Air France's regular Boeing 747 schedule could achieve by flying supersonic. Air France had gained immense experience of Concorde commercial operation and the Boston flight was an important prerequisite to obtaining approval to fly the most vital route of all: Paris to New York's JFK. The cloud hanging over transatlantic scheduled Concorde services was the passing in the US of the 1969 Environment Protection Act.

Air France's first commercial Concorde service was flown on 21 January 1976 from Paris to Dakar and on to Rio, the flight crew being Captain Pierre Chanoine, First Officer Pierre Dudal and Flight Engineer André Blanc. Meanwhile the extended and often acrimonious hearings, chaired by the US Department of Transport's Secretary General William T. Coleman, Jr, concluded on 4 February 1976 that Air France could commence schedules to both Washington-Dulles and New York JFK. Air France planned to commence Paris-New York Concorde schedules on 15 March, though this was delayed by further objections by the Port of New York Authority (PoNYA) over fears of noise and environmental impact. Judge Pollack presided over a protracted hearing, ruling on 17 August 1977 that PoNYA's objection to Concorde had been 'excessive and unjustified as well as discriminatory, arbitrary and unreasonable'. It was not until 22 November that the first Concorde services to JFK commenced.

By 14 June 1978, Air France's Concorde fleet had carried its 100,000th passenger, a Monsieur Walter Lang who was making his fifteenth supersonic Concorde flight. The following year on 12 January, Air France's Concorde

One of the first two Boeing 747-128s, F-BPVB, was delivered to Air France in April 1970, featuring the airline's 1950s and 1960s dark blue and white colours. F-BPVB remained in service with Air France until 1994. With the 747, Paris was just eight hours away from New York, compared to the twenty-four hours and two stopovers when the service first started in June 1946. (*GPJ Collection*)

schedule to Washington-Dulles International was extended to Dallas in Texas in a code-share arrangement with Dallas-based Braniff International Airways. In an unusual piece of bureaucracy, the Concordes had to change their registration from F-B—- to N—— at Washington before the onward flight to Dallas; for example F-BVFC became N94FC.

France's Caribbean territories (Guadeloupe, Martinique, Marie Galante, Désirade, and St Barthélemy) plus French Guiana (Cayenne) were a regular destination for transatlantic operations from Paris, notably Pointe-à-Pitre in Guadeloupe and Fort de France in Martinique. 1974 saw the introduction of Air France's first two Boeing 737-247's (N4504W and N4522W) both leased from Western Airlines and used for services linking the major island airports, Cayenne and Miami in Florida. It wasn't until 1983 that

Air France's own Boeing 737s were introduced to its European network.

The 1970s, Air France fleet, Concorde excepted, was a mix of indigenous and Boeing designs. By 1978, it numbered 102 aircraft (excluding the Postale de Nuit F.27s and Transalls). As well as the continued and extensive use of Caravelles, Airbus A300B2 and B4 aircraft were starting to be used. Boeing 707-328s were still in extensive use and the Boeing 727-228 fleet had grown to number twenty. Boeing 747 'classics' were also now in widespread use, both 747-128s and 747-228s, some of the latter being freighters. The first 747-128s entered service on 9 April 1970 (F-BPVA and F-BPVB), followed by the more powerful, longer range 747-228s. The Air France 'widebody' fleet – Boeing 747s and Airbus A300s – increased from just four 747s in 1970 to twenty-two aircraft by 1975 (comprising fifteen B747s and seven A300s). Over the same period, the number of staff employed by Air France worldwide grew from 27,588 to 30,312 – a far cry from the 2,501 employed at the airline's formation in 1933.

On 23 May 1974, another new era opened – Air France inaugurated its Boeing 727s on the Paris to London

Above: Another of the early batch of Boeing 747-228Bs delivered during the 1970s, F-BPVY joined Air France in April 1979 and was still active with the airline when pictured crossing the 'bridge' at Paris Orly in July 2003. (GPJ)

(Heathrow) route and in 1974 its first Airbus A300B2 F-BVGA flew its first commercial service to London on the same route, in a flying time of just 51 minutes. This aircraft was to remain in service for twenty years, until October 1994.

1974 was also the year for a major image change. The airline's livery, which had remained virtually unchanged since the end of World War II received a makeover: an iconic livery still in use and still contemporary today. The new livery featured blue, white and red stripes of varying thicknesses on aircraft tails, with the remainder of the aircraft white, save titles. Air France's use of the former Air Union 'hippocampe' seahorse logo was now consigned to history.

Another historic event had occurred in December 1969: the signature of a pool agreement between Air France, Aeroflot and Japan Air Lines which also enabled Air France to overfly the Soviet Union to Far East destinations. Services commenced on the Paris-Moscow-Tokyo route on 9 April 1970.

Below: F-BPVL Boeing 747-128 was originally registered N88931 when delivered in March 1974, but assumed its French registration later. It was also one of the airline's 747s to be emblazoned with 'jumbo' on the rear fuselage, the 747 having aquired the name 'jumbo jet' soon after being introduced. (*GPJ Collection*)

Above: In the sort of approach that in 2008 is totally unacceptable, Air France's Boeing 727-228 F-BPJK leaves a trail of black emissions behind it on finals to land at London Heathrow in July 1974. (*AIC*)

Below: An unusual Air France lease in summer 1973 was the Douglas DC-8-32 OO-TCP (c/n 45265), shown here at Orly in June 1973. Originally a Pan American Airways aircraft, in 1973 it was owned by Pomair and subsequently went to Capitol International as N900CL. (*MJH*)

Concorde's arrival at any airport in the 1970s attracted thousands of sightseers, in what seemed a hark-back to the 1950s. This is the visit of Air France Concorde F-BVFD to Cardiff-Wales airport (formerly Rhoose) to operate a charter flight on 21 October 1979, the first time Concorde had visited Cardiff. A former Cambrian Airways DH.89 Dragon Rapide was parked alongside Concorde to illustrate how radically air transport had changed in little over thirty years. (*GPJ*)

Left: Aérospatiale Concorde F-BVFA set two world speed records for Air France in 1978 on commercial routes. (*AFM*)

Above: Concorde F-BVFA on take-off when scheduled transatlantic supersonic services between Paris and Washington DC commenced on 24 May 1976. (*AFM*)

Above: Airbus A300s quickly became the mainstream equipment on many of Air France's busy European routes during the 1970s. F-BVGO is seen here producing dramatic wing-tip vortices in a wet-weather take-off at Cardiff International airport whilst operating a weekend rugby international charter. (*GPJ*)

Left: The first Air France Airbus A300 schedules were from Paris to London Heathrow where this example, F-BVGF (delivered in June 1975), is pictured in June 1978 in Air France's 'old colours'. This aircraft joined Air Inter's fleet in 1983. (*GM*)

Above: In the Air France colours of the 1950s and 1960s, in which it was delivered in March 1969, Boeing 727-228 F-BPJI taxies at Paris Charles de Gaulle in May 1977. (*GM*)

Below: Boeing 747-128 N28903 was delivered to Air France as a leased aircraft (hence US registration) in February 1973. It is seen here at Paris Charles de Gaulle in May 1977 and became F-BPVJ in December 1981. (*GM*)

Above: One of the first of Air France's Boeing 707-328B fleet to receive the airline's new livery, *Chateau de Dampierre* F-BLCD pictured in May 1977 at Paris Charles de Gaulle; the aircraft joined the Air France fleet in February 1966. (*GM*)

Below: Painting of Concorde F-BVFA over New York (note the Twin Towers) by Philippe Mitschké to celebrate the 22 November 1977 arrival of the first Paris to New York supersonic Concorde schedule. (*AFM*)

F-BTSD (c/n 213), which also wore the US registration N94SD for a brief period in 1979, operated Concorde services for Braniff International onwards from Washington to Dallas, Texas. (*Aviation-Images.com*)

air france

The Concorde era, which so epitomised French style and chic, was the ideal opportunity to mix French fashion and cuisine with the world's only supersonic scheduled air services (British Airways excepted). Bernard Ingrand represented the lucky designer Jean Patou for the first uniforms worn by Air France Concorde air hostesses, but Nina Ricci was also recruited in 1985.

With membership of SkyTeam, the privatisation of the airline and merger following merger, Air France decided in 2001 that their Madame Carven designed uniforms, originating from the mid-1980s, needed a huge revamp.

MAIN FRENCH AIRLINE UNIFORM DESIGNERS 1971-2008

1971 Jacques Esterel
for Air France

1973 André Courrèges
for UTA

1976 Jean Patou
for the Air France Concorde

1976 Maison Rodier
for Air France

1978 Carven, Nina Ricci and Grès
for Air France

1979 Hermès
for UTA

1985 Nina Ricci
for the Air France Concorde

1986 Christian Dior
for UTA

1987 Georges Rech
for Air France
Nina Ricci, Carven and Louis Féraud
for Air France

2005 Christian Lacroix
for Air France

Above: The Paris couturière Carven was chosen by Air France to design these two hostess uniforms in 1978. (*AFM*)

Air France appointed a four-person team 'to work full time on the ambitious project.... and invest fully in this new creation'. A budget of 20 million euros was allocated. Christian Lacroix's company, founded in 1987 and quickly becoming one of France's fashion icons, was chosen to design the new Air France uniforms. There were 31,000 meetings to take staff measurements, 100 separate items designed by Lacroix, 650,000 items manufactured, 1 million square metres of fabric ordered, and all to clothe the 36,000 staff members (25,000 women and 11,000 men) who would now wear the new uniforms

Above: These Air Inter hostess winter uniforms were worn from 1962 to 1969, and for the introduction of Air Inter's first Caravelle services, designed by Georgette de Trezes. (*GPJ Collection*)

Left and Above: What a hemline and what colour! Reminiscent more of a US West Coast airline than a provincial French airline, but nonetheless part of Air Inter's bid for publicity and traffic in 1969, designed by Jacques Esterel. The introduction of these uniforms coincided with the inauguration of Air Inter's Dassault Mercure fleet. (*GPJ Collection*)

'to symbolise French elegance… while showing an openness to other world cultures'.

The introduction of the new uniform in 2005 followed on the heels of the formation of the new Air France-KLM Group created in May 2004, now widely acknowledged as the world's leading air transport group in terms of turnover and number three worldwide in terms of revenue passenger kilometres.

Right: With Concorde came ultimate 'chic': these three styles of hostess uniform designed by Nina Ricci and introduced in the mid-1980s. (*AFM*)

Far left and Left: Contrast the uniforms in these two sets of Louis Féraud-designed outfits introduced in 1987: the dark suits for 'winter' operations and the cotton dresses for 'summer'. (*AFM*)

Below: Introduced by Air France in 2005, Christian Lacroix was the chosen uniform designer for both flight-deck and cabin crew. (*Air France Photo*)

Boeing 727-228 F-BPJI, delivered to Air France in March 1969, part of a batch of five delivered at this time, and pictured here on approach to London Heathrow in August 1988 shortly before it was retired from service and sold in November 1989, becoming N601AR with Key Air. (*MJH*)

7

1980s
Upheaval

These were a continuation of the
difficult times Air France suffered in
the 1970s. The US dollar was under
considerable pressures, hampering the
world economy, and industrial unrest
surfaced at home in France. The last
Air France Caravelle flight (F-BHRY,
Touraine) took place on 1 April 1981,
the type being replaced following the
placing of an order for Boeing 737-200s.

1980s

DELIVERY OF THE FIRST BOEING 737-200 FROM SEATTLE, F-GBYA, CAME IN DECEMBER 1982. AS WELL AS THE 737S IN 1984, AIR FRANCE ALSO ADDED THREE AIRBUS A310S TO ITS FLEET. THE VIABILITY OF CONCORDE SERVICES TO SOUTH AMERICA WAS ALSO QUESTIONED AND THESE WERE ULTIMATELY WITHDRAWN ON 1 APRIL 1982.

Paris-Charles de Gaulle airport at Roissy, which had been opened on 8 March 1974, was expanding fast as Air France's international home, and in June 1982 Terminal Two at CdG was commissioned and opened. The terminals at CdG or Paris Nord, as it was originally known, were designed by architect Paul Andreu, construction of the new airport having begun in 1966.

The early 1980s also saw the retirement of the last Boeing 707 from Air France service and by 1983 the airline's total fleet numbered ninety-nine aircraft: seven

Concordes, thirty-one Boeing 747s, twenty Airbuses, twenty-nine Boeing 727s and twelve Boeing 737s. These totals exclude the aircraft of Postale de Nuit and those of associate company Air Charter International (ACI), which had four Boeing 727s, about ten Caravelles and the Boeing

Boeing 747-228B F-GCBD (ex N1305E) completes a non-stop Paris to San Francisco flight in the late 1980s, mixing it with US domestic traffic (Alaska Airlines) and a rival French charter flight of Minerve (DC-10 F-GCNZ). (*GPJ*)

737s of partner charter companies. By the 1980s, Air France had an 80% stake in ACI, the remaining 20% held by Air Inter. ACI served traditional European Mediterranean holiday destinations, plus Scandinavia, the US and Canada. ACI's livery was also updated in March 1981, with just the 'ACI' initials and the Air France and Air Inter names alongside. With the exception of its Boeing 727s, all ACI's aircraft were now leased, the Caravelles from Europe Aero Service (EAS) of Perpignan and the Boeing 737-200s from Euralair.

On 5 March 1983, Air France's first Boeing 737-228, F-GBYG, became operational, part of the airline's major fleet modernisation plan with twelve of the type ordered. After the deep recession of 1982, 1983 saw Air France on the road to recovery in time for its 50th anniversary. By this time it employed 34,600, had a fleet of ninety-nine aircraft and a route structure totalling 634,400kms (391,605 statute miles) serving 150 destinations in 73 different countries worldwide. In comparison with other European airlines, Air France now ranked 'number two' in terms of both international passengers (behind British Airways) and freight (behind Lufthansa). It ranked fourth in the world for passengers. From this, the 1980s developed into a period of growth and profit.

In February 1987, Jacques Friedmann became Air France's President and in June launched his *Projet Air France* to help further revitalise the airline. In July 1987, he took the bold decision to order seven of the new long-range, four-engine Airbus A340, with options on a further four. He also signed a deal with Boeing on 16 December for sixteen Boeing 747-400s to be delivered between 1991 and 1996, placing options on a further twelve aircraft. After only nineteen months, *Projet Air France* was suspended and Friedmann stepped down as Air France's president, being replaced in October 1988 by Bernard Attali. In a period of management upheaval, Jean-Didier Blanchet also replaced Henri Sauven as Director General in March 1988.

On 26 March 1988, the first Airbus A320-100, F-GFKA, was delivered to Air France, entering service on 18 April on the Paris-Düsseldorf-Berlin route, plus services to Amsterdam and Frankfurt. The excitement about the first 'fly-by wire' A320 was severely tempered with the crash on 26 June of an Air France A320-110, F-GFKC, performing at an air show organised by the Mulhouse Flying Club at Mulhouse-Habsheim. The investigation committee concluded that the accident – in which the three crew on board, the only

Below: Touching down on London Heathrow's runway 28R in the early 1980s, Air France Airbus A300B4-2C F-BVGJ. A300s were used for many years on the prestige Paris-London route. (*GPJ*)

occupants, were killed – resulted from a combination of very low fly-over height, very low speed with maximum possible angle of attack, engine speed at flight idle and late application of go-around power. This combination of factors led to an impact with trees, causing the fatal crash.

The first Airbus A320-200 was delivered in August 1989, followed by the first of four Boeing 747-400s –

a further order for seven Airbus A340-300s was also placed. The first of a small fleet of Airbus A310-304s entered service on 9 November 1989, F-GEMO being the first of these, flying a Paris-Strasbourg-Lyons-New York service on 9 November. Between 1986 and 1989, Air France's international passenger numbers grew by 11.5%, fully justifying its investment in new, long-range aircraft.

Right: One of the first of Air France's initial batch of twelve Boeing 737-228s, F-GBYC, delivered in the first half of 1983 as a Caravelle replacement and pictured at Geneva in June 1986. (*MJH*)

Right: A rugby international 'air-lift' at Cardiff's Rhoose airport in 1984 by Air Charter International (ACI) Boeing 727-228 F-BPJR. This aircraft had been delivered to Air France in February 1972 before being transferred to the ACI fleet. (*GPJ*)

Left: King of Air France's long haul fleet for over a decade, the Boeing 747-428, F-GISB is seen here on the familiar curved approach to Hong Kong's Kai Tak airport in July 1996. (*GPJ Collection/Pierre-Alain Petit*)

Below: During 1987 and 1988, Air France's first revolutionary 'fly-by-wire' Airbus A320s were delivered. F-GFKG, an A320-111, *Ville d'Amsterdam* was one of these early deliveries, seen here on a wet and windy day at Zurich, Switzerland, in April 1993; still in service in 2008, now with twenty years' service to its credit. (*GPJ*)

Airbus A320-211 F-GFVD, which Air France Europe (successor to Air Inter) leased from Guinness Peat Aviation Group during the 1990s, seen nosing into its stand at London Heathrow in November 1997. (*GPJ*)

8

1990s

Consolidation and Privatisation

(Air Inter & UTA)

On 12 January 1990, the operations of all French government-owned airlines, Air France, Air Inter, Air Charter International and UTA, were merged into the new Air France Group, losing their individual identities over the next few years as the mergers came to practical fruition. The 1990s were the turning point for Air France, changed from Government ownership to a privatised company.

1990s

A NEW HOLDING COMPANY GROUPE AIR FRANCE WAS SET UP BY GOVERNMENT DECREE ON 25 JULY 1994 AND IMPLEMENTED BY 1 SEPTEMBER 1994. IT HAD A MAJORITY SHAREHOLDING IN BOTH AIR FRANCE AND AIR INTER, WHICH HAD BEEN RE-NAMED AIR FRANCE EUROPE. HOWEVER, THE GROUP WAS STILL NOT RUN ON FULLY COMMERCIAL LINES, WITH POLITICAL INFLUENCE AND DEMANDS FOR STATE HAND-OUTS STILL RIFE.

The period 1991 to 1993 was another era of investment in new equipment. Fourteen additional Boeing 747-400s were ordered to replace the 747-100s, many of which were now twenty years old. A single Airbus A310-300 and Boeing 767-300 were added and the first Airbus A340s entered service. Twelve Boeing 737-500s, featuring between 100 and 120 seats, were ordered for medium size markets, complementing the twenty-eight Airbus A320s in the fleet. The first twin-engine Airbus A330s arrived, and the first dedicated Boeing 747-400 freighter. By 1993, the average age of Air France's fleet was 8.3 years, compared to 10 years in 1990.

Christian Blanc was Chairman and CEO of Groupe Air France and established an almost unprecedented level of support from everyone from politicians to the company's own employees, in trying to turn the airline around. He led an initial public offering (IPO) but was thwarted following the French elections in 1997 when the country swung to the left. In October, Blanc resigned, the IPO was put in abeyance and after a short while former Air Inter boss

Boeing 737-33A F-GHVN, an ex-UTA aircraft, pictured at Paris Orly airport in June 1995. (*MJH*)

Air Charter Airbus A320-211 F-GFKX in the airline's new colours operating a weekend charter from Nantes Atlantique airport in May 1995. (*GPJ*)

Jean-Cyril Spinetta was appointed Chairman and the privatisation process was re-ignited. By 1997, Air France Europe had been fully absorbed into Air France and the last vestiges of Air Inter had disappeared.

Another name that had been established over thirty years, Air Charter International (ACI) also disappeared in October 1998 when the wholly owned Air France subsidiary ceased operations and became part of Groupe Air France. By this time ACI had a fleet of five A320s, one A300B4, two A310-324s and two Boeing 737-200s.

Major elements of the privatisation plan included cost control, the development of Charles de Gaulle airport as a hub operation, the consolidation of domestic services to meet the growing threat from low-fare airlines and finally, Air France's joining of a major world airline alliance.

The previously belligerent employees started to toe the party line, despite wage concessions, productivity deals and rationalisations in numbers. The 'carrot' was the opportunity for them to take an equity stake in the company. It wasn't all plain sailing as the 1998 strike proved, but the integration of Air France Europe (formerly Air Inter) and UTA enabled the 'new' airline to shed 23%

of its routes, many of which were prestigious or traditional routes, but which never stood a chance of being profitable.

Fleet modernisation was also in full swing. In 1995, Air France's fleet (excluding aircraft acquired from Air Inter and UTA) totalled 168 aircraft (excluding Postal de Nuit aircraft), a mix of mainly Airbus and Boeing types. Two Douglas DC-10-30s, a surplus of the UTA merger, were also on fleet and also the six Aérospatiale/BAe Concordes. The Boeing 727 fleet had now been disposed of, with the exception of one example being leased to Air Gabon. The last 727 schedule was flown between Tel Aviv and Paris Orly on 31 October 1993. Airbus types included the A300, A310, A320 and A340, most numerous type being the twenty-nine examples of the A320. Boeing types included 737 and 747 'classics', plus the first 747-400s and seven Boeing 767-200 and 300ERs.

Air France also experienced strike action. During summer 1998, just as the nation was preparing to host the

Epitomising Air France's global reach, this classic shot of Boeing 747-228M F-GCBF on very short finals over the beach on the approach to St Maarten in the Leeward Islands, West Indies. (*Mark Wagner/aviation-images.com*)

1990s

World Cup (soccer), Air France's pilots' union staged a walk-out. At the time Air France was trying to negotiate the equity participation scheme among pilots in the upcoming privatisation of the airline. The pilots returned to work the day before the World Cup kicked off, although their dispute was not resolved until November, having the effect of reducing the airline's net profitability by at least half a billion francs and forcing the privatisation to be delayed until the following year. On 10 February 1999, the French government partially privatised Air France on the Paris stock exchange.

1999 was also the start of the process to merge the currencies of eleven of the European Union countries, a process that came to fruition with circulation of the new Euro coins and notes in France on 1 January 2002. This was a crossroads time for Air France because it was also trying to decide whether to enter a global alliance with either Delta Air Lines or Continental in the USA.

On 9 April 1998, Air France inaugurated its first Boeing 777-228 service. F-GPSA was the first aircraft and flew the service from Paris to New York. They replaced Boeing 747s and in some instances Airbus A340s. Subsequently Boeing 777s replaced – occasionally supplemented – Airbus A340s on the airline's service to Delta's major hub at Atlanta, Georgia, USA.

In 1998, Air France was one of the world's largest airlines, second in terms of aircraft maintenance, third in terms of international air freight and fourth in terms of international passenger transport. The airline served 281 destinations in 88 countries and flew 35.6 million passengers during the year. It weathered the summer-time strike very well, turning a record profit. The impending privatisation helped to impose a degree of financial discipline and conservatism that had previously been lacking in the company. At privatisation, Air France also acknowledged that in the next five to seven years, the majority of its aircraft fleet would need to be replaced. The privatisation was a clever way of avoiding payment of as much external debt as possible, and was also beneficial in furthering Air France's attempts at fiscal discipline.

On 22 June 1999, Air France and Atlanta-based Delta Air Lines signed a partnership agreement. This would pave the way to the formation of the SkyTeam global alliance in June 2000. It also enabled the two carriers to compete more effectively against some of the other up and coming airline alliances that were springing up: the One World and Star Alliances.

This Boeing 777-228IGW F-GSPA was the first to join the Air France fleet in 1998. It is seen here operating at SkyTeam partner Delta Air Lines' Atlanta hub in June 2003. (*GPJ*)

Above: Airbus A340-311 F-GLZG at pushback from the gate at Delta Air Lines' Atlanta hub. (*GPJ*)

Below: Mainstay of Air France's short and medium haul services in the 1990s were its fleet of Airbus A320s, plus other 'family' types, the A321 and A319. F-GHQK, delivered to Air France in August 1991, is seen here at Amsterdam Schiphol. (*GPJ*)

Air Inter

AIR INTER WAS FOUNDED IN FRANCE ON 12 NOVEMBER 1954 AS SOCIÉTÉ ANONYME DES LIGNES AÉRIENNES INTÉRIEURS (AIR INTER) BY SEVERAL BANKERS AND A GROUP OF INVESTORS FROM THE AIR TRANSPORT INDUSTRY (AIR FRANCE, UAT, TAI, AIR ALGÉRIE, AIGLE AZUR AND SNCF). THE INITIAL CAPITAL WAS ONE MILLION 'OLD FRANCS', AND THE FIRST PRESIDENT WAS EDOUARD CATALOGNE. HOWEVER, IT TOOK NEARLY THREE AND A HALF YEARS FOR THE NEW COMPANY TO ASSEMBLE A 'BUSINESS PLAN' AND OBTAIN ALL THE NECESSARY PERMISSIONS FROM THE MINISTRY OF PUBLIC WORKS, TRANSPORT AND TOURISM TO ENABLE THEM TO OPERATE THEIR FIRST SCHEDULED FLIGHT. AIR FRANCE ACQUIRED A 24% STAKE IN AIR INTER IN 1955. DURING THIS TIME AIR INTER OPERATED CHARTER FLIGHTS USING A VARIETY OF AIRCRAFT LEASED FROM OTHER AIRLINES.

In 1953, Douglas DC-6B F-BGOC became the first aircraft to wear the Air Inter colours, a former Transports Aériens Intercontinentaux (TAI) aircraft. Another TAI DC-6, F-BHVA, was used, as well as one of TAI's DC-3s. Air France aircraft were also chartered including Lockheed L-749 Constellation F-BAZF and DC-3 F-BEIF.

On 16 March 1958, Douglas DC-3 F-BFGX flew the airline's first schedule from Strasbourg to Paris (flight number IT011) carrying local dignitaries, airline officials (including the airline's then President, René Lemaire) and members of the press.

On 24 March, using a UAT Douglas DC-4, the inaugural Paris-Marseilles service was flown followed on 2 April and 18 May respectively by new DC-3 (TAI aircraft) services from Paris to Bordeaux and Lyons. Lyons was planned to become the focal point of Air Inter's services. In 1958, Air Inter also pioneered an 'executive' helicopter service (using Alouette II, F-BIFL) linking Paris's two main airports at Orly and Le Bourget. Other early seasonal services were also flown from Paris to Dinard, Vittel and La Baule. However, these early forays

into scheduled air passenger services were terminated by October of 1958 because of insufficient resources. In 1960, 'The Admiral' Paul Hébrard took over the presidency of Air Inter and re-launched the airline to serve destinations in metropolitan mainland France plus Corsica. Whilst there was considerable pressure to purchase the new turbo-prop Fokker F.27 Friendship, Air Inter resisted.

It wasn't until 1 October 1968 that the first of thirteen F.27s joined the Air Inter fleet. Instead, in 1960 Air Inter acquired the former Airnautic Vickers Vikings F-BJEQ and F-BIPT – these were first used on a Pau-Paris (Orly)-Pau service, promoted by the Pau Chamber of Commerce.

TAI Douglas DC-3 with Air Inter logo on its nose. (*GPJ Collection*)

This was followed in December by new services to Nice, Marseilles, Lyons and Nantes. Other services from Paris to Toulouse, Brest and Perpignan followed in May 1961. An Air Paris DH.114 Heron 1, F-BGOJ, was also used by Air Inter at this time.

Initially as an experiment, promoted mainly by French aircraft manufacturer Nord Aviation, Air Inter started to use a Nord 262 Super Broussard on its Paris (Orly)- Nantes schedule – in fact the predecessor to this design, the Nord 260 was used on this route for a while. The Potez P.840 was also considered by Air Inter. Four 29-passenger Nord 262s (F-BLHS, F-BLHT, F-BLHU and F-BLHV) were subsequently purchased for Air Inter's secondary routes that could not support the larger Viscounts which had joined the Air Inter fleet in 1962. They were retired from service at the end of 1968.

A joint Air France/Air Inter operation on the Paris-Nice route was inaugurated on 1 April 1961. Under the exclusive name of Air Inter, the revamped airline's first schedule, metropolitan flights using Vickers V.708 Viscounts (acquired from Air France), took place on 1 April 1962 from Paris (Orly) to Nîmes and Paris (Orly) to Clermont-Ferrand. The formation of a new *société* by the French government, incorporating Air Inter and charged with flying a domestic scheduled air services network, separate from Air France, was considered a bold, and in some quarters, a controversial decision. SNCF, the nationalised French railway system was a continuous critic of the expansion of Air Inter. Orly-Sud terminal also became the adopted Paris 'home' for Air Inter.

The operation with Viscounts was followed in 1964 by service with Caravelles. Two Air France Caravelle IIIs began twice daily Air Inter operations on the Paris (Orly) – Marseilles route, beginning on 6 March. By 15 May, a third

Above: Douglas DC-6B F-BGOC (c/n 43834) was delivered to TAI in May 1953 but immediately transferred to Air Inter with which it operated charters until 1958. (*GPJ Collection*)

Below: A group of charter passengers, headed by Air Inter President René Lemaire, who had been flown on a summer-time Air Inter service from Paris to La Baule (Escoublac) in 1958. (*GPJ Collection*)

wet-leased Caravelle had been added, Air France supplying the flight-deck crew and Air Inter the cabin crew. By 1966, Air Inter was operating Caravelles on its scheduled services from Paris (Orly) to Lyons, Toulouse, Bordeaux, Nice and Nîmes. A July 1965 order by Air France for two Caravelle IIIs was transferred to Air Inter under a lease/purchase agreement following the May agreement by the French government to renew Air Inter's operating licence for a further twenty years. Further Caravelle IIIs were ordered.

From that time on, Air Inter grew rapidly. In 1962, it had carried 100,000 passengers, 5 million by 1968 and 30 million by 1975. This was despite considerable competition from its main rival, the French Railways, SNCF. In a major expansion of routes during 1965/66, Air Inter boosted its geographical coverage of France with 52 scheduled routes (all year and seasonal) and including the start of services to Corsica.

By 1970 Air Inter's fleet numbered seventy aircraft, Fokker F.27-500s, Viscount V.708s and 724s and Caravelle IIIs. The first 'Super' Caravelle 12s didn't arrive until October 1972.

Air Inter were also looking for a larger capacity, short haul jet. Boeing offered their 727-200, but at the end of 1969 Air Inter decided to place options for ten of Avions Marcel Dassault's new 134-passenger twin-jet, the Mercure. It wasn't until 30 January 1972 that Robert Vergnaud, Air Inter's President and Director General, actually signed a firm order for the ten aircraft. The prototype Mercure's (F-WTCC) maiden flight at Bordeaux Mérignac was on 28 May 1971. Air Inter wanted first delivery on 30 October 1973, but the programme slipped by six months and the

Air Inter acquired four 29-passenger Nord 262s, introducing them on the Paris to Nantes service. F-WLHS (c/n 4), pictured pre-delivery, became F-BLHS. (*MJH*)

airline had to acquire Caravelle 12s to make up the shortfall in capacity. The inaugural Air Inter Mercure schedule (F-BTTA) was on 14 June 1974 between Paris (Orly) and Marseilles, and return.

Air Inter's launch of its new 'flagship' short haul jet also saw the airline introduce striking new, predominantly red, uniforms for its flight attendants (see Chapter 6). Between 1962 and 1969 Air Inter flight attendants had worn 'couture' designed blue uniforms created by Georgette de Trezes. Jacques Estérel designed the dramatic new red uniforms that formed the basis of the airline's flight attendants' apparel between 1969 and 1985. Women played an important part in Air Inter's history. The airline's first female Captain was appointed in 1966 – 19 years later, on 7 February 1985, an all-female crew flew Mercure F-BTTB between Paris and Nîmes – Anne-Marie Peltier was Captain, Bridgitte Lescop 1st Officer and Colette Vibert Flight Engineer. Cabin crew were Michèle Ancelot, Corinne Bourret and Murielle Poulet.

Always apparently supporting the French civil aviation industry in a fiercely competitive environment, Air Inter ordered three new Airbus A300-B2s on 24 December 1975. They were intended for its most prestigious and busiest routes, services from Paris to Lyons, Marseilles and Nice, with Toulouse to be added later. F-BUAG flew Air Inter's

Left: Air Inter's first scheduled flight was operated between Strasbourg and Paris on 17 March 1958 using an Air France Douglas DC-3 F-BFGX. (*GPJ Collection*)

On 24 June 1982, Robert Vergnaud retired as Air Inter's President, replaced by Marceau Long on 10 July. The competition that Air Inter experienced from surface transportation acquired a new dimension when the first TGV (Train à Grande Vitesse) service between Paris and Lyons was inaugurated on 27 September 1981. Almost immediately Air Inter's traffic on this route dropped by 28%. Air Inter's main base was at Paris (Orly), and the airport's operator ADP set about a major revamp of Air Inter's terminal at Orly-Ouest, coinciding with the airline's order for the new, smaller Airbus A320. Their first aircraft, F-GGEA, was delivered in January 1988. One of the biggest disasters to befall Air Inter was the 20 January 1992 crash of A320-111 F-GGED, when it hit high ground during a bad weather approach to Strasbourg with the loss of all 87 on board.

first A300 schedule on 29 November 1976. Eventually Air Inter operated a fleet of twenty-two Airbus A300s, sixteen of the B2 version and six of the larger B4 versions that could carry up to 314 passengers. In July 1977 Air Inter took a 20% share in associate airline Air Charter International, a charter operator set up by Air France.

Towards the turn of the century, and before the demise of Air Inter and its assimilation into Air France, four famous French couturiers were appointed to design new uniforms (see Chapter 6): Paco Rabanne, Christian Lacroix, Jean-Louis Scherrer and Emanuel Ungaro. Air Inter and its management regarded their flight attendants as an essential ingredient of the passenger's flight experience, but also as a vehicle to promote French fashions – the female flight attendants were called *Les ambassadrices de la mode française*.

Right: Historic photo on the anniversary of Air Inter's epoch-making 1962 introduction to service of Vickers Viscount turbo-prop aircraft. Left to right Monique Delaunay, Monique Britsch, Paul Marland, Chief Executive, or 'The Admiral' Paul Hébrard, M. Bailly, Gérard Brandeis, Albert Dubreuil, Thérèse Révellin. (*GPJ Collection*)

In 1989, the reorganisation of the French airlines started to take effect. Firstly UTA – whose roots went back to 1937 – and Aéromaritime became part of Air France, which formally became Groupe Air France. At the same time, now under the presidency of Jean-Cyril Spinetta, Air Inter was also brought under the same umbrella, along with UTA and Air Charter International. The Mercure epoch at Air Inter ended on 29 April 1995 at Paris (Orly) when Captain Bernard Sanson landed the last scheduled Mercure (F-BTTB) flight. For over 20 years the jet had performed without major incident, the ten aircraft fleet having accumulated 360,815 hours and carried out 430,916 landings, including the pioneering of a British-designed auto-land HUD (head-up display) system for landings in fog and poor visibility. The experience with the Mercure in poor visibility was important in the development of a similar system for the airline's A300 fleet. 97% of the Mercure's departures had been on time. F-BTTB was donated to the German air museum at Speyer, others being distributed around France to museums and technical colleges.

The first of the thirty-seven Airbus A320s that were to fly with Air Inter entered service with the airline in January 1988. These were joined by five of the larger Airbus family, the A321 in mid-1994. Airbus A319s we introduced in mid-1996, nine of the type being ordered. The majority of these aircraft later joined the Air France fleet.

On 17 January 1994 the first of Air Inter's General Electric-powered Airbus A330s, F-GMDB, was put into service on the Paris to Marseilles route, and by July Air Inter had four of these 412-seat configuration Airbus aircraft in service – the A330s replaced Airbus A300s on this route and provided 25% more carry-on baggage space than the A300. Air Inter's Airbus A300 fleet flew an estimated 550,000 hours in the course of 455,000 flights transporting 95 million passengers during the twenty years of service.

Air Paris DH.114 Heron 1 F-BGOJ was used on Air Inter services in the late 1950s before the airline started to acquire its own aircraft. (*GPJ Collection*)

Air Inter Europe Airbus A321-111 (c/n 0544) F-GMZE pictured at Basel/Mulhouse in March 1996 wears the basic colours of Air France but with Air Inter Europe titles. This aircraft was soon assimilated into the Air France fleet with which it still operates in 2008. (*GPJ*)

In 1992, the first A300s started to be retired from the fleet and by 1997 they had all but disappeared from service, replaced by both smaller Airbus A320s and larger A330s. Three of Air Inter's A300 fleet, F-BUAK, F-GBEA and F-GLOC, soldiered on and were not retired until April 2000.

The changes experienced by Air France had profound influence on Air Inter and the whole French airline industry. Michel Bernard became Air Inter's President when Spinetta departed in October 1993. He oversaw roll-out and service entry of the first Airbus A330s but survived only until May 1995 when Christian Blanc took over. In 1994, Air Inter carried 17.055 million passengers, but with deregulation in France, new airlines such as AOM, Air Liberté and TAT (franchised with British Airways) provided fierce competition, particularly at Paris (Orly) and in Air Inter's markets at Bordeaux, Toulouse, Marseilles, Strasbourg and Montpellier.

Blanc launched his new 'survival' project, Air Inter Europe, on 5 October 1995. All branding, including the colours of its aircraft were changed to Air France colours. It was effectively, apart from by name, 'Air France Europe'. By 1996, the competition from other airlines had become even more fierce and development of the TGV network continued, predicted to be within three hours of half the French population by 2002. Air Inter Europe was carrying 17 million passengers per annum.

European 'open skies' became a reality on 1 April 1997. On 12 September 1997, the French Assembly General formally approved the full merger of Air France and Air Inter and the name that had had been a symbol for French domestic air transport for 35 years disappeared for ever. In an ironic twist of fate, it was Air Inter's former President, Jean-Cyril Spinetta, who took over as the President of the considerably enlarged Air France on 22 October 1997, a post he still holds in 2008. On 1 April, the Air Inter fleet, which comprised thirty-five Airbus A320s, five Airbus A321s, five Fokker F.100s and nine Airbus A319s, was harvested by Air France and the vestiges of another famous French airline disappeared for ever.

Above: Air Inter
Vickers V.708
Viscount F-BOEB
parked at Paris
Orly.
(*GPJ Collection*)

Right: Crossing the
characteristic
'taxiway bridge' at
Paris Orly in the
spring of 1971,
Air Inter V.708
Viscount F-BGNT.
(*GPJ Collection*)

Above and above right: Two images of Air Inter's first manual card booking system at its Orly headquarters in 1962. (*GPJ Collection*)

Below: Air Inter Caravelle III F-BNKH on the apron at Cardiff's Rhoose airport in March 1976 operating a French rugby airlift charter – this aircraft was one of the first batch of Caravelles ordered by Air Inter and delivered in 1967 and 1968. It ceased operations in January 1983 and was scrapped at Orly in 1985. (*GPJ*)

Right: Air Inter's mid-1980s route structure embraced the whole of mainland France plus its three Corsican destinations: Bastia, Calvi and Ajaccio. (*GPJ Collection*)

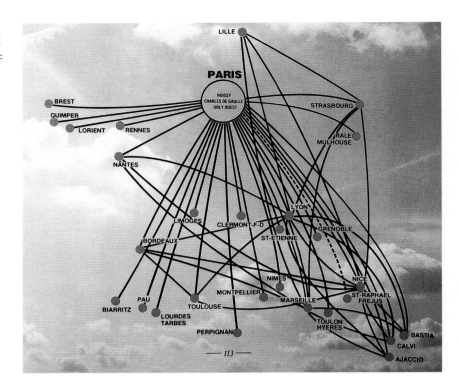

Below: Air Inter's Paris headquarters at Orly-Nord during the 1960s. (*GPJ Collection*)

Left: Air Inter operated a total of twenty-three different Airbus A300s in its fleet between 1976 and the mid-1990s. F-BUAJ (delivered to Air Inter in February 1980) is seen here on short finals to land on runway 36 at Perpignan airport in June 1991 at the end of one its twice-daily services from Paris Orly. (*GPJ*)

Left: First all-female crew on the Paris to Nîmes schedule on 7 February 1985. Left is Anne-Marie Peltier (Captain), Bridgitte Lescop (Pilot) plus Colette Vibert (Flight Engineer). Aircraft F-BTTB Mercure also had Chief Hostess Michèle Ancelot and two other hostesses, Corinne Bourret and Murielle Poulet, aboard. The first Air Inter female captain was Jacqueline Dulut in 1966. (*GPJ Collection*)

Right: F-BTTA Mercure 100 (c/n 01) lifts off from Calvi's sloping runway 36 on the Mediterranean island of Corsica in October 1987. (*GPJ*)

Below: As part of the Christian Blanc survival project in 1995 and the launch of Air Inter Europe, aircraft started to appear in a variety of schemes. This Air Littoral Fokker 70 PH-RRS, seen in November 1995 at London City airport, sports joint Air France/Air Inter 'Express' titles for its scheduled services to Paris Charles de Gaulle. (*GPJ*)

Union de Transports Aériens (UTA)

THE ROOTS OF THIS FAMOUS INTERNATIONAL FRENCH AIRLINE EXTEND BACK TO 1948 AND THE FORMATION OF SOCIÉTÉ AÉRIENNE DE TRANSPORTS INTERCONTINENTAUX (SATI). USING THREE WAR-SURPLUS CONSOLIDATED VULTEE B24 LIBERATOR BOMBERS, CONVERTED INTO A COMBINED PASSENGER/FREIGHT CONFIGURATION, ONE OF THEIR FIRST TASKS WAS IN THE RELIEF OF A FRENCH POLAR EXPEDITION HEADED BY EXPLORER PAUL-EMILE VICTOR, WHICH WAS STRANDED IN GREENLAND WITHOUT SUPPLIES. ON ANOTHER FLIGHT, A SATI LIBERATOR THEN ESTABLISHED A NEW LONG DISTANCE RECORD ON 6 DECEMBER 1949, WHEN A CREW OF FIVE (VEILLARD, FALLOU, MONTRET, CHANUT AND MISS FRETTE-DAMICOURT) FLEW NON-STOP FROM FRANCE TO CAYENNE, FRENCH GUIANA, IN 25 HOURS AND 55 MINUTES, A TIME REDUCED BY 30 MINUTES ON THEIR RETURN.

SATI became Union Aéromaritime de Transport (UAT) in 1949. The original Aéromaritime had been founded in 1935 by the shipping company Chargeurs Réunis under the supervision of Francis Fabre, which operated mainly Sikorsky S.43 seaplanes to provide a service between Dakar and Pointe-Noire. This Aéromaritime became part of Air France in 1941 (see Chapter 3). UAT operated feeder services in West Africa, New Caledonia and other French overseas territories using a fleet of nine de Havilland DH.114 Heron 1Bs, including F-OANS, displayed at 1961's Paris Air Show in a joint UAT/Aéromaritime livery. UAT also ordered Douglas DC-8-32s, the first one, F-BJLA, delivered on 27 June 1960, and quickly adopting the same joint UAT/Aéromaritime livery; F-BJLB followed on 5 August.

Transports Aériens Intercontinentaux (TAI) was founded in 1946 and operated in parallel with UAT, concentrating on international services from France to French dependencies not served by Air France, particularly in Africa and south-east Asia (Saigon). In 1956 TAI took over all of Air France's services from France to West, Central and Southern Africa. The two rival independent airlines, UAT and TAI, merged on 1 October 1963 under the presidency of General Georges Fayet as Union de Transports Aériens (UTA), a private company serving destinations in West Africa, (with the exception of Dakar) and the French islands in the South

Pacific (New Caledonia, Fiji, Tahiti), linking them to the west coast of the USA (via Papeete), New Zealand and Australia. UTA's fleet was initially Douglas DC-6s and DC-7s: DC-6 F-BHMS was destroyed and all seventy on board killed on 2 October 1964 when the aircraft flew into Mount Alcazaba in Spain whilst flying a schedule from Palma de Mallorca to Port Étienne (now Nouadhibou) in Mauritania.

In 1965, UTA ordered two Caravelle 10Bs for use in Africa and the South Pacific, based respectively in Paris and at Nouméa, New Caledonia. The first UTA Caravelle, F-BNRA, went into service on 21 February 1966 on the Paris-Nice-Tripoli schedule, later expanded to routes serving Bordeaux and Marseilles, with destinations including Ouagadougou, Bobo Dioulasso, Abidjan, Conakry and Bamako, with Las Palmas as an intermediate technical stop. The Nouméa-based Caravelle was F-BNRA, replaced temporarily by F-BOEE from Africa, and this entered service on the schedule to Sydney, Nadi and Auckland in December 1966. Douglas DC-8s (series 53 and 62) displaced the Caravelle on UTA's West African services in summer 1971. F-BNRA was phased out of UTA services by DC-8s in 1974 and early 1975, its last duties including some forty evacuation missions to save 3,600 French nationals from Saigon at the time of the US withdrawal from Vietnam. Those evacuated were ferried to Phnom Penh, Cambodia.

The next UTA fleet acquisitions were five Douglas DC-10-30s and subsequently the lease of two further DC-10-30s from the manufacturer. UTA's order with McDonnell Douglas was expedited through its membership of the KSSU group, formed in 1967 as an alliance of DC-10-30 launch customers KLM, SAS and Swissair, which UTA joined in 1970 (KSSU was a rival group to the ATLAS alliance of European airlines founded in 1969 by Alitalia, Lufthansa, Air France and Sabena, joined in 1972 by Iberia). The DC-10-30 had General Electric CF6-50 engines and the prototype first flew at Long Beach, California, on 21 June 1972. First delivery of a DC-10-30 to UTA was on 18 February 1973.

Following Fayet's retirement in 1969, Francis Fabre took over the presidency of UTA until 1981, when René Lapautre was appointed. He saw the airline through to the end of its 27-year history in 1990, preceding the airline's purchase by Air France, completed the following

year. By 1988, UTA was serving 50 destinations on five continents. One of the worst accidents in air transport history occurred on 19 September 1989 when one of UTA's leased Douglas DC-10-30s, N54629, flying on a Brazzaville-N'Djamena-Paris (Charles de Gaulle) schedule was destroyed by terrorist action over Niger when an on-board bomb was detonated. All 156 passengers and 15 crew were killed.

UTA grew to be the largest independent French carrier, wearing the stylish and unmistakable green, white and blue livery. When it was taken over by Air France in October 1991, the UTA DC-10s and two Boeing 747-400s were assimilated into the Air France fleet and the DC-10 briefly wore the national carrier's livery for the first time.

One of nine UAT/Aéromaritime's DH.114 Heron 1s (F-BGOI, c/n 14010) on delivery in 1953 at Douala, Cameroon. (*MJH*)

This and overleaf: Sikorsky S.43s were flown by Compagnie Aéromaritime from December 1936 onwards on its Dakar-Conakry service. The 16-passenger amphibians were later used to extend Aéromaritime's coastal service to Pointe-Noire with stopovers at Abidjan, Cotonou, Douala, Libreville and Port Gentil. (*MJH*)

Above: Fine air-to-air picture of the SE.2010 *Armagnac* F-BAVD in Transports Aériens Intercontinentaux (TAI) colours. In 1962, TAI and UAT merged under the name Union de Transports Aériens (UTA). (*MJH*)

Right: Le Bourget scene in the mid-1950s with a UAT DC-6B F-BGSN, which the airline acquired in September 1955, and behind Vickers Viking G-AJCE of UK charter airline Independent Air Transport. (*via Georges Grod*)

Left: UAT/Aéromaritime DH Comet 1A F-BGSB, one of three the airline ordered, pictured at Hatfield in January 1953 prior to delivery to Paris for the airline's pioneering jet service to Dakar and Abidjan in West Africa. (*MJH*)

Left: UAT Douglas DC-6A F-BGTY (c/n 43818) was delivered in April 1954 but here mysteriously wears Cyrillic script titles at Le Bourget in May 1957. (*MJH*)

Left: Paris Orly in the early 1960s with the TAI Douglas DC-8-31 F-BIUZ (c/n 45570) also wearing Air France titles (F-BIUY was the other DC-8-31 delivered to TAI at the time). F-BUIZ was delivered in February 1961 and transferred to UTA's fleet in October 1963 before assignment to the Armée de l'Air as F-RAFE in 1973. (*DC*)

Left: When Airbus Industrie started using its fleet of four Super Guppy 201s to transport Airbus parts between European factories, Aéromaritime was charged with the operation – this Guppy is pictured at Manchester Ringway in 1982. (*GPJ*)

Below: Mainstay of UTA's fleet prior to the take-over by Air France were the Boeing 747-400 (nearest, F-GETA) and the Douglas DC-10-30 (N54649). (*GPJ Collection*)

Left: UTA also operated a cargo division with the Boeing 747-228F F-GCBM (c/n 24879) – prior to this it had used F-GBOX and three 'combi' 747s. The aircraft is pictured at Miami, Florida, in January 1991. (*GPJ Collection/ Hans-Werner Klein*)

Below: UTA's Boeing 747-400 F-GEXA acquired the nickname *Big Boss*. (*GPJ Collection*)

Air France took a 25% equity stake in CityJet in May 1999
in partnership with Air Foyle Ireland and acquired the airline
outright in February 2000. One of CityJet's growing fleet of
BAe146 and RJ-85s is seen on approach to Zurich, Switzerland,
in March 2007. (*GPJ*)

9

Other Associate Airlines

(including Regional,
CityJet and Brit Air)

Transport Aérien Transrégional (TAT),
formerly Touraine Air Transport, based at
Tours in the Loire Valley, was the first
airline to wave the Air France flag in
what became known as 'franchising'.
The airline remained independent but
operated services on behalf of the
'major', in this case Air France and even
wore the Air France logo. Later the
aircraft were painted in full Air France
colours with just a small 'TAT' logo.

TAT WAS FOUNDED IN 1968 BY MICHEL MARCHAIS, BEGINNING WITH CHARTER FLIGHTS BEFORE INAUGURATING SCHEDULES USING BEECHCRAFT QUEEN AIR 65S BETWEEN TOURS AND LYONS IN DECEMBER 1969. TAT ABSORBED THE OPERATIONS OF AIR ROUERGUE, AIR ALPES AND AIR ALSACE (WHICH WAS ONE OF THE FEW AIRLINES TO OPERATE THE GERMAN-DESIGNED VFW-614 TWIN-JET IN COMMERCIAL SERVICE). WITH ITS FIRST FOKKER F28 FELLOWSHIP ARRIVING IN APRIL 1974 IN FULL AIR FRANCE COLOURS, TAT STARTED TO FLY A NUMBER OF ROUTES UNDER CONTRACT TO AIR FRANCE BASED ON LYONS. TAT ALSO FLEW BEECHCRAFT 99S AND FAIRCHILD-HILLER FH-227BS, SOME IN ITS OWN DISTINCTIVE YELLOW LIVERY, BUT OTHERS IN AIR FRANCE COLOURS. IN 1995, TAT SIGNED AN OPERATING AGREEMENT WITH LILLE-BASED FLANDRE AIR, OPERATING THEIR BEECHCRAFT BE1900CS ON TAT SERVICES.

Several other French 'local' airlines have been assimilated into Air France to become wholly owned subsidiaries. These are: Régional (based in Nantes), CityJet (based in Dublin) and Brit Air (based in Morlaix). There have been several other airlines who have had associations or code-shares with Air France to fly 'thinner' routes on contract. Jersey European (now Flybe) operated a significant code-share alliance with Air France between 1997 and 2003 using their BAe146 jets,

several painted in full Air France colours, notably to operate on the London Heathrow to Toulouse schedule. Another British airline, Newcastle-based Gill Airways, received its first

TAT had become France's premier regional airline by the early 1980s, surpassing even Air Inter, and serving over fifty domestic destinations. First joining TAT during 1980, its fleet of Fairchild-Hiller FH-227s numbered twenty aircraft. F-GCPT is pictured here on a charter to Guernsey in September 1987. (*GPJ*)

Right: The evolution of the TAT livery
to an almost 100% Air France livery
is depicted here in the late 1980s
on Fairchild-Hiller FH-227 F-GCLN
when visiting Guernsey. (*GPJ*)

ex-Midway Airlines Fokker 100s in the
summer of 1999 and introduced them
on its Newcastle to Paris schedule,
operating in full Air France colours.
By 2000 Gill Airways had expanded its
Air France franchise partnership to fly
services from Humberside, Newcastle
and Teesside (now Durham Tees Valley) to Paris as well as
two 'wet-lease' routes from Paris to Gothenburg and
Helsinki. After surviving 'administration', Gill Airways
ceased operations in September 2001.

Other airlines wearing the Air France colours to a greater
or lesser extent included many of France's small regional
airlines in the 1980s and 1990s, such as Air Alsace and
Protéus Airlines. Farther afield EuroBerlin France was set up
jointly by Air France and Lufthansa and operated a fleet of
seven Monarch Airlines Boeing 737-300s on services from
Berlin's Tegel airport between 1988 and 1994, initially to
Düsseldorf, Hamburg and Stuttgart. The aircraft remained
UK registered and were flown by Monarch crews. On 17
October 1989, EuroBerlin carried its 500,000th passenger,
and by 6 June 1990 topped the one million mark on a flight
between Cologne/Bonn and Berlin. Three additional aircraft
were added, including two ex-Aéromaritime Boeing 737-
300s for the winter season 1990/91.

Services to Munich, London Gatwick and Naples were
added and EuroBerlin also operated charter flights on
behalf of Air France. There were proposals to reposition the
airline to a UK base such as London Stansted, but this never

Below: Following its first flight in October 1988, Brit Air were
one of the first customers for the ATR-72-201 and took delivery
of this aircraft, F-GHPU (c/n 227) and F-GHPV (c/n 234) in
1991. These supplemented its much larger fleet of nine ATR-42s,
two of which flank the ATR-72 at Rennes in this March 1992
photograph. (*GPJ*)

materialised. The last EuroBerlin flight was flown on 30 October 1994 from Naples to Berlin, as the two airline owners failed to find a suitable new economic model for the airline and decided to go their own ways.

Air Littoral, the Montpellier-based French regional that started operations in 1972, had an alliance with Air France and Air France Europe, operating Fokker 70s on Air France/Air Inter Express services in Europe (see Chapter 8). Air Littoral went bankrupt in 2004. Lille-based R-Lines was a short-lived Beechcraft Be1900D operator around 2000 that wore the Air France colours and flew schedules to Angers (Marcé) and Clermont-Ferrand. Airlinair (in which BritAir has a 19.5% shareholding), the Paris Orly-based airliner wet-lease specialist, also flies ATR-42s and 72s for major carriers including Air France and wearing the full Air France livery. Air France has an 11.95% stake in Corsica-based CCM Airlines (Compagnie Corse Mediterranée) and has developed an important partnership, the airline now flying a mix of Airbus A319s and ATR-42 and 72s from the three main Corsican cities of Calvi, Ajaccio and Bastia to points on the French mainland. CCM dropped the Air France livery in favour of its own distinctive identity with the delivery of new ATR-72s in 2006.

Régional was formed in 2001 as a wholly owned subsidiary of Air France, but its history, through its predecessor airlines Flandre Air, Protéus Airlines and Regional Airlines goes back much farther. The first Regional Airlines was formed on 1 January 1992 with the amalgamation of French regional carriers, Air Vendée and Airlec with a varied fleet that included BAe Jetstream 31s, Fairchild Metro IIIs and Saab 340Bs. Flandre Air was established by the Delesalle family as a charter airline in 1977 based in Lille (Lesquin). Scheduled services were started in 1985 and they flew a fleet of Beechcraft Be1900Cs and 1900Ds, Embraer EMB.120s and in October 1997 became the European launch customer for the Embraer RJ-135 regional jet. Flandre Air became an Air Liberté franchisee in November 1998. Protéus Airlines were established in 1996 based at Dijon (Bourgogne) and started scheduled services in May, building a hub at Lyons with over 70 flights a day to French domestic destinations. They flew a fleet of Fairchild Dornier 328-100s and Beechcraft Be1900Cs and Be1900Ds and were to be the launch customer for the Fairchild Dornier 328JET. In August 1997, they signed a franchise agreement with Air France.

CityJet, with operations based in Dublin, Ireland, was founded in January 1994 by Patrick Byrne. Its initial focus

Below: By 17 October 1989, after less than a year of operation, EuroBerlin had boarded its 500,000th passenger on the EE5145 flight from Stuttgart to Berlin. (*GPJ Collection*)

Below right: EuroBerlin's Boeing 737-300 G-MONN pictured at Berlin Tegel airport, one of seven ex-Monarch Airlines 737s they operated. (*GPJ Collection*)

was a scheduled service between Dublin and London City airport using a fleet of BAe146-200 regional jets. In May 1999, in partnership with Air Foyle Ireland, Air France took a 25% stake in CityJet and since February 2000 CityJet has been a wholly owned subsidiary of Air France. It has expanded to operate seven routes (Paris Charles de Gaulle to Dublin, Florence, London City, Birmingham, Edinburgh, Gothenburg and Zurich) on a franchise basis for Air France, now with a fleet of 17 BAe146s. CityJet also leases aircraft and crew to Air France. In January 2007 CityJet introduced its first of more than twenty ex-Mesaba Airlines (Northwest Jet Airlink in the US) Avro RJ85s, part of an expansion from April 2007 for the airline at London City (with services to Belfast, Dublin, Dundee, Edinburgh, Geneva, Madrid, Milan, Nice, Paris and Zurich), Dublin and Paris.

In September 2007, CityJet absorbed Scot Airways' UK regional scheduled routes from London City, with some Dornier 328-110s being painted in the Air France livery.

Brit Air became a wholly owned subsidiary of Air France in October 2000 and now employs over 1,200 personnel, operates over 260 daily flights linking 40 cities in France and Europe, operates an all-jet fleet of forty-one aircraft

Remaining loyal to Bombardier, Brit Air ordered the larger CRJ-700 and 701LR when it needed larger aircraft. It operates 260 daily flights including to London Gatwick using these CRJ-700s.

that include Bombardier CRJ-100ERs, CRJ-700s and Fokker 100s from its main hubs at Lyons St Exupéry (LYS), Paris Orly and Paris Charles de Gaulle. Brit Air is still based at Morlaix in Brittany.

In 2006, Air France-KLM announced that the KLM subsidiary Transavia would be used as a way of entering the low-cost market at Paris Orly-Sud. A French-registered company bearing the name Transavia was formed and some of the Boeing 737-800s of Transavia were transferred to the new company. By summer 2007, Transavia (France) was operating to nine destinations, planned to increase to sixteen by mid-2008. Air France-KLM also have a 50% ownership stake in Amsterdam-based Martinair (AP Moeller Maersk own the other 50%) and during 2007 were reported to be trying to acquire a majority shareholding. KLM had previously tried to acquire Martinair in 1998 but this acquisition was blocked.

Right: Jersey European Airways (JEA), now Flybe, entered a code-share alliance with Air France in 1997 and soon became a franchisee, operating Air France Express services with their fleet of BAe146s, including G-JEAT (Srs100), seen here on approach to London Heathrow in March 1997. (*GPJ*)

Below: CCM ATR-72 (F-GKPC) on short finals to land at Calvi in Corsica in June 2004. Note the bandit's head on the engine cowling, a distinguishing feature from the otherwise full Air France livery. However, more recently CCM has chosen to re-introduce its own identity, although Air France still hold a 11.94% stake in CCM and there is still a code-share alliance between the two airlines. (*GPJ*)

Above: UK regional airline Gill Airways, based in Newcastle, operated Air France franchise services between 1999 and 2001 using three leased Fokker 100s G-BYDN, G-BYDO (pictured) and G-BYDP. (*TD*)

Left: Regional Airlines was based at Nantes Atlantique airport in western France and quickly grew a fleet of BAe Jetstream 32s and Saab 340Bs. At the time of this picture, in August 1993, this Jetstream F-GMVL was one of six of the type that had just joined its fleet. In 1996, Regional Airlines was jointly owned by Air Exel (14%), Airlec (14%), Air Vendée (60%) and Air Transport Pyrenees (12%). (*GPJ*)

Air France (right) was one of the four founder members of the
SkyTeam alliance in 2000 along with Delta Air Lines (USA),
Aeromexico and Korean Air. (*GPJ Collection*)

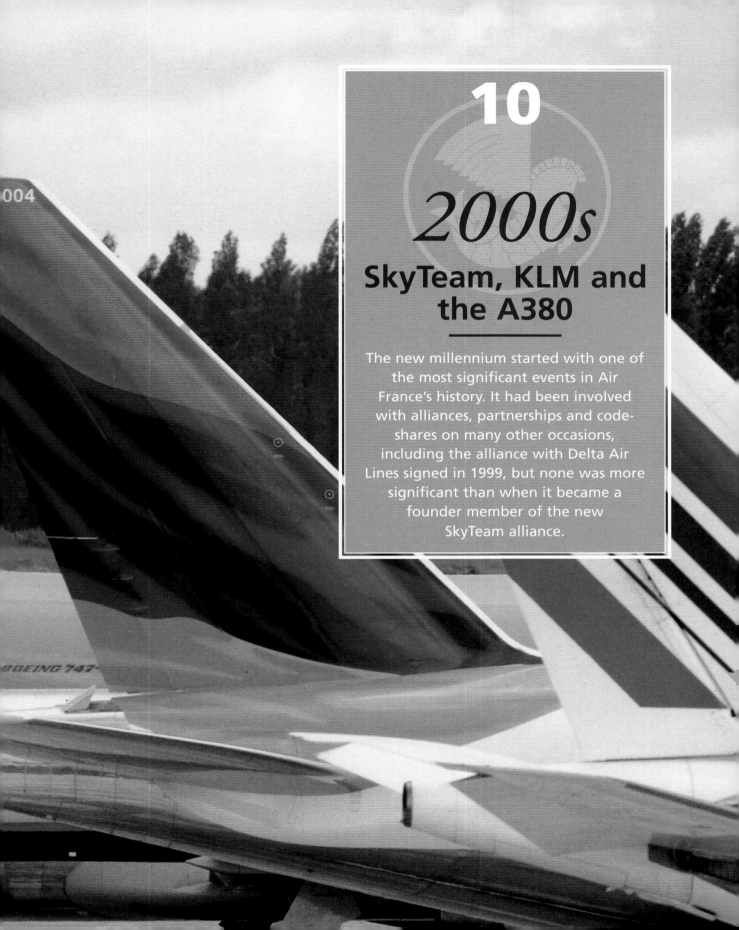

10

2000s

SkyTeam, KLM and the A380

The new millennium started with one of the most significant events in Air France's history. It had been involved with alliances, partnerships and code-shares on many other occasions, including the alliance with Delta Air Lines signed in 1999, but none was more significant than when it became a founder member of the new SkyTeam alliance.

2000s

THIS WAS A DEEPER AND MORE PROFOUND THAN ANY IT HAD PREVIOUSLY BEEN INVOLVED WITH, THE FOUNDING ALLIANCE AIRLINES BEING AIR FRANCE, DELTA AIR LINES, AEROMEXICO AND KOREAN AIR, WITH AN AGREEMENT FINALLY SIGNED ON 22 JUNE 2000. IT WAS A FORMAL, BUSINESS-LED REACTION TO OTHER MAJOR WORLD AIRLINE GROUPINGS: ONE WORLD AND THE STAR ALLIANCE. IT ALSO ACHIEVED ONE OF THE FOUR MAIN OBJECTIVES SET BY CHRISTIAN BLANC AT THE TIME HE EMBARKED ON THE FIRST IPO IN 1997.

The SkyTeam alliance bought several world hubs firmly into the Air France timetable, notably Seoul Inchon, Atlanta Jackson Hartsfield and Mexico City. The Air France logo appeared extensively at all these diverse locations on departure and arrival boards, with many of the member airlines now operating flights with joint flight numbers. With Air France as part of SkyTeam, this alliance was transporting 174 million passengers per annum and had a combined main-line passenger and cargo fleet of 985 aircraft.

More recently, on 28 June 2007 SkyTeam member airlines, which now number ten – Aeroflot Russian Airlines, Air France, Aeromexico, Alitalia, Continental Airlines, CSA Czech Airlines, Delta Air Lines, KLM Royal Dutch Airlines, Korean Air and Northwest Airlines – applied to the US Department of Transportation (DOT) for anti-trust immunity for their transatlantic services. Included in the application is a joint venture agreement between Air France, Delta, KLM and Northwest that would create a comprehensive and integrated partnership among these four SkyTeam members across the Atlantic. The application is the first following the landmark European Union-US open skies treaty which aims to create a fully liberalised air transport market place worldwide. Anti-trust immunity offers considerable advantages to passengers with more choice of flight

Airbus A318 F-GUGA, the smallest of the A320 'family' of single-aisle airliners – Air France's first example was delivered in October 2003. (*Airbus photo*)

End of an era at Paris Charles de Gaulle airport: 31 May 2003 saw the last commercial Air France Concorde flight. (*Nigel LePage*)

schedules, travel times, services and fares. The Northwest-KLM alliance was the first to be given anti-trust immunity by the DOT as long ago as January 1993.

As part of the open skies agreement Air France will relinquish some of its valuable London Heathrow "slots" to enable SkyTeam partner Delta its first ever access to Heathrow for schedules to Atlanta and New York JFK. Air France will also fly a direct Heathrow to Los Angeles schedule using Boeing 777s.

On 28 June 2007, Air France-KLM signed a preliminary agreement with China Southern Airlines with the intention of the latter joining the SkyTeam alliance. Air France-KLM have been independently strengthening their presence in China, including a new cargo venture (see Chapter 3). On 1 July 2007, Air France-KLM introduced two extra services between Paris and Shanghai, increasing to twelve the number of services per week they operate on this route.

2003 saw the end of an era with the retirement of Air France's supersonic Concorde services. The disastrous crash of flight AF4590 at Gonesse on 25 July 2000, when Air France Concorde 203 F-BTSC experienced a tyre burst

during take-off from runway 26R at Paris Charles de Gaulle airport and crashed 8 kilometres to the west of the airport killing all 109 people on board, was a seminal moment. Air France and British Airways grounded all Concorde flights immediately, although BA recommenced Concorde services the following day. On 14 August, the French Bureau Enquêtes Accidents (BEA) announced that Concorde's Certificate of Airworthiness had been suspended and the British Civil Aviation Authority (CAA) followed suit. Concorde had been flying for almost 25 years, with the fleet achieving 84,000 flight cycles and 235,000 flying hours. Amongst the nine crew killed in the crash were Captain Christian Marty, First Officer Jean Marcot and Flight Engineer Gilles Jardinaud.

Air France was less than enthusiastic about returning Concorde to commercial service, even though the French had already established a commission to study an environmentally

acceptable successor to Concorde. The cause of the crash was quickly established as a metal strip deposited on the runway from the thrust reverser of a DC-10 that had taken off immediately before Concorde. This had punctured a tyre causing pieces of the tyre to be thrown against the Concorde's structure. A major fire ensued.

BA and Air France set August 2001 as a target date to have their Concorde fleet back in the air. After extensive investigation, evaluation and engineering, a modification 'fix' was established. On 17 July 2001, BA Concorde G-BOAF departed London Heathrow on its first post-Gonesse test flight. By 7 November 2001, Concordes went back into service with BA on the London to New York (JFK) route and Air France on the Paris to New York (JFK). In a re-enactment of the two airlines' May 1976 first commercial services to New York, the Concordes of the two airlines were posed nose-to-nose, with Air France's Captain Edgard Chillaud joining BA's Captain Mike Bannister. The revival of commercial Concorde service was short-lived. On 10 April 2003 Air France announced that its Concorde fleet would be withdrawn from service on 31 May. 24 October was chosen

Illustrating one of Europe's most important and successful commercial airline mergers ever, the forming of the Air France-KLM Group in May 2004, this KLM Boeing 737-800 and Air France Airbus A320 pass each other at Amsterdam's Schiphol airport in June 2006, one of the two important hub airports dominated by the Air France-KLM Group. (*GPJ*)

by BA as its final day for Concorde commercial service.

Air France's post 9/11 fortunes were not as disastrous as some other airlines which had a higher proportion of transatlantic schedules. It succeeded in rapidly shifting capacity on its transatlantic schedules and one year on had achieved nearly a 14% reduction in seat kilometres offered whilst dropping only one US destination, Dallas-Fort Worth. In contrast it increased its African capacity by 69%, albeit partly due to the demise of both Swissair and Sabena in these markets.

Air France has always championed technical innovations as far as its aircraft fleet is concerned, but unlike some major world airlines has not confined its airliner orders to just one of the 'big two' – Boeings sit comfortably with Airbuses in the Air France fleet. Airbus family aircraft are nonetheless the backbone of Air France's short and medium haul fleet with A318, A319, A320 and A321 aircraft. It is the long haul fleet that is more diverse and complicated. Boeing 767s were retired in the winter of 2002 and the last of the small fleet of Airbus A310-304s made its final Beirut to Paris flight on 14 April 2002 after the type had been in service for nearly thirteen years. Fourteen new Airbus A330-200s replaced the ageing Airbus A310-200 and 300 fleets. 2002 was also the start of retirements for the Air France Boeing 747-200s, whilst new Boeing 777-200s and 777-300ERs (for which Air France was the launch customer) started to join the Air France fleet.

On 9 October 2003, Air France took delivery of the first of fifteen 123-seat Airbus A318s – the 'baby' of the A320 'family' – which it had originally ordered in April 1999 as European launch customer. Frontier Airlines in the US was the first to put the A318 into service. The first aircraft, F-GUGA, was the 2,035th member of the A320 'family' to be delivered by Airbus and the 119th to join the operational fleet of Air France. The last new one entered service in December 2006, when the airline's final Boeing 737-500 was retired.

The most historic event of Air France's recent history, and possibly of its entire 75-year existence, occurred in 2003 and 2004. On 30 September 2003, Air France and KLM Royal Dutch Airlines announced a merger through a share exchange, together with an agreement for KLM to join the SkyTeam alliance. By May 2004 Air France and KLM had completed their merger with this share exchange and officially became the Air France-KLM Group. Each airline retained its individual brand, but with passengers able to benefit from co-ordinated schedules throughout their entire route network. In December 2004, the French state sold 18.4% of its equity stake in the Air France-KLM Group, reducing its holding to 18.6%.

As of 31 March 2007 the merged airlines have a combined fleet of 575 aircraft (165 long haul, 222 medium haul and 188 in their regional fleet), were operating flights to 247 destinations in 104 countries worldwide and employed 102,000 people. They had two prominent European hubs at Paris Charles de Gaulle (7th largest airport in the world in terms of passengers) and Amsterdam Schiphol (12th largest in the world). By the end of the current decade the Air France-KLM Group hope that their

return on capital investment will reach their declared 7% target. During the second half of the decade efficiencies and savings were being actively sought, including the premature phasing out of all their ageing, fuel-guzzling Boeing 747-200 'classics' (cargo and passenger versions) by the end of 2007. This was not originally planned until 2009. With the price of fuel an ever-present thorn in their side, the Air France-KLM Group managed to hedge fuel prices for 2007 and 2008.

In comparison with the Air France-KLM figures above, Air France itself has a fleet of 383 aircraft, including 127 belonging to regional subsidiaries. SkyTeam currently has a fleet which numbers 2,018 aircraft plus another 1,190 aircraft of subsidiaries. The ten SkyTeam airlines fly 15,000 daily flights to 728 destinations in 149 countries and carry 373 million passengers annually.

Delays in the delivery of Air France's initial order for ten Airbus A380s (with four options) have also been a significant problem, the Group hoping that the introduction of new, more fuel efficient types with lower maintenance costs would help significantly towards their efficiency drive and boost their financial performance.

In 2007, Air France-KLM planned a 5.6% growth in their long haul network, including a 10.1% boost to the North American market – this latter growth is mainly attributable to the 11 June start of a direct Paris to Seattle schedule using Airbus A330-200s. Other international growth areas are Latin America (11.4%) and Asia (7.3%). In summer 2007, Air France-KLM also boosted their medium haul network with a 4.3% capacity increase. Boeing 777-300ERs replaced the airlines' Boeing 747-400s on services to the French Caribbean and to Réunion. The last of Air France's Boeing 737s (a Srs500 aircraft, F-GJND) was also retired on 11 June, the end of a 25-year period of service for this Boeing twin-jet, making short haul services the exclusive preserve of Airbus types. The last Air France Boeing 737 service, flown by the Head of Air France's 737 Division Captain Eric Monlouis, was a flight from Turin to Paris Charles de Gaulle. In contrast at KLM, all its short haul flights are operated by Boeings, and it is adding new examples to its fleet.

Air France-KLM is incorporated under French law and based at Roissy-Charles de Gaulle Airport, Paris. It is the largest airline in the world in terms of operating revenues, the largest in Europe and third largest in the world measured by passenger kilometres. Chief Executive Officer (CEO) is Jean-Cyril Spinetta, the ex-Air Inter boss and former CEO of Air France prior to the merger. Private shareholders now own 81.4% of the company, the remaining 18.6% being retained by the French government.

The most recent financial figures, for the financial year 2006/07, were announced by Air France-KLM Chairman Jean-Cyril Spinetta on 23 May 2007. Spinetta said at the time that the past year, '…has demonstrated the benefits of our profitable growth strategy. We have taken advantage of global growth to develop our business in all major markets and increase our profitability through cost control while continuing to invest in our future.' In real terms the Air France-KLM revenues were up 7.6% to 23.07 billion euros, while operating income was up 32.5% to 1.24 billion euros, all in all a 7% return on capital employed. This also boded well for the future, with an 8.5% target return on capital employed for 2009/10 being predicted. Air France-KLM now move in to the second phase of their joint development, along with a new cost saving phase of greater integration, known as 'Challenge 10'. It has the objective of achieving 1.4 billion euros in savings over the next three years (up to 2010), bringing unit costs down by 3%. These steps should help Air France-KLM offset a declining fuel-hedge position and combat continuing oil price rises.

With the announcement of the 2006/07 figures in May 2007, Air France Group's Chief Operating Officer Pierre-Henri Gourgeon also announced new aircraft orders and a compensation deal following Airbus A380 delivery delays. Thirty more Airbus A320 and A321 single-aisle types have been ordered (eighteen purchased and twelve leased), plus thirteen more Boeing 777-300ER 'wide bodies' that will replace all passenger Boeing 747-400s by 2013; a further five Boeing 777-200Fs will be purchased to replace Boeing 747-400F freighters. Two more A380s were also added as part of the Airbus compensation deal, bringing Air France's total A380 order to twelve aircraft, with two options. No details were revealed on the price that Air France paid for these two aircraft. Air France's first three A380s are due to join their fleet in spring 2009, with three more a year in each of the subsequent years.

Airbus A330-203 F-GZCB taking off on its delivery flight from Toulouse. (*Airbus photo*)

Above: Evening picture of Airbus A320-211 F-GHQP (c/n 0337) landing at Basle/Mulhouse. (*Airbus photo*)

Left: Airbus A319 taking off still carrying its German test registration D-AVYF, later becoming F-GRHR with Air France. (*Airbus Photo*)

Computer-generated image of an Airbus A380
in Air France colours. The first is scheduled
for delivery in Spring 2009. (*Airbus Photo*)

A beautiful portrait of Air France Airbus A340-300 F-GLZM (c/n 237)
lifting off on another long haul flight. (*Airbus photo*)

BIBLIOGRAPHY AND FURTHER READING/REFERENCE

Air Inter – Du XXème au XXIème siècle by Alain Ayache, published by Les Meilleures Éditions, 75016 Paris in 1988

Airlife's Airliners: 9 – AIRBUS A320 by Tim Laming and Robert Hewson, published by Airlife, 2000

Boeing 707/720 – Airlife's Classic Airliners by Jim Winchester, published by Airlife, 2002

Caravelle – The Complete Story by John Wegg, published by Airways International, Inc, 2005

Delta Air Lines – 75 Years of Airline Excellence by Geoff Jones, *Images of America* series published by Arcadia in the US, 2003

DC-1 DC-2 DC-3 The First Seventy Years by Jennifer Gradidge, published by Air Britain, 2006

Icare (Revue de l'Aviation Française) – Air France et Son Histoire: Première Partie 1933-1959 (No.106) and *Air France et Son Histoire: Deuxième Partie 1960-1983 (No.107)* edited by Jean Lasserre

Icare (Revue de l'Aviation Française) – Air France et Son Histoire 1933-2003 – Troisième Partie 1983-2003 (No.185 and No.186) edited by Jean Lasserre

Icare (Revue de l'Aviation Française) – Air Inter Tome 1 (No.168) by Jean Lasserre

Registre France 1920-1985 by Pascal Brugier, published by Le Trait d'Union, 1985

The Big Six US Airlines by Geoff Jones, published by Airlife, 2000

The Concorde Story: 21 Years in Service by Christopher Orlebar, published by Osprey Publishing, 2002

The Lockheed Twins by Peter J. Marson, published by Air Britain, 2001

Un Siècle d'Aviation Avec AIR FRANCE by Jean Lasserre et Hélène Le Guernevé for Musée Air France, 2000